Financial Due Diligence For Commercial Real Estate

Proven Methods to Detect & Prevent Fraud

Second Edition

By

Jerold Ipsen, CFE, MBA

Table of Contents

Introduction

The Internet has become a double-edged sword. While much of the information we desire is readily available, the bad guys who wish to do us harm continually discover new ways to take our money. This concept is especially true of those involved in real estate transactions. To lessen the impact, conscientious investors routinely conduct due diligence to verify information and uncover discrepancies such as material overstatements and unrevealed facts. The first edition was primarily directed towards buyers, lenders, and brokers desiring to learn more about financial due diligence as it applies to commercial real estate. In the second edition, the audience has expanded to include developers and insurers, and the focus has turned toward methods used to commit commercial real estate fraud.

For the due diligence practitioner, seasoned or those new to the field, and for those interested in learning more about fraud in commercial real estate, I have added several topics:

Money Laundering

- Why little has been done involving overseas money and commercial real estate purchases?

Wire Fraud:

- Beware of hackers finding their way into real estate transactions.

Commercial Real Estate Fraud: Fraudulent schemes include:

- Misrepresentation
- Misappropriation of Funds
- Non-Disclosure
- Document Forgery
- Phony or Inflated Appraisals
- Bank Insiders and Collusion
- Illegal Property Flipping
- Short-Sale Schemes
- Advance Fee Schemes

- Multi-Family Mortgage Fraud
- Purchase Transaction Fraud.

In the second edition, I want to call attention to the unscrupulous people who see the Internet as an opportunity to misrepresent themselves with the intent to perpetrate a scam. For example, on several popular websites, it is the aim of many good, hardworking people looking to connect and network. Nevertheless, many of the same sites (without the ability to vet every member) also provide a platform to many who portray themselves as knowledgeable professionals, but are not. This edition addresses those people who are scammers, looking to take your money. In the past, concern about internet security primarily focused on misrepresentation. However today, with internet theft on the rise, the focus is now on hackers breaking into email and payment accounts in an effort to separate people from their money.

Fraud, greed and deceit has a way of finding those who are willing to do or say anything to close a real estate deal. Methods described here include examples of overstating one's capabilities, the inflation of assets, lack of financial stability, imminent bankruptcies or the borrower's past to include credit problems, pending civil litigation and criminal actions.

In writing the second edition, and to do the subject justice, I needed to address such topics as: money laundering, wire fraud, advance fee schemes, multi-family mortgage fraud, and the consequences of those who use these methods.

Financial Statements

Removing the unknowns by providing necessary and truthful information remains an integral part of the due diligence process. The second edition addresses this fact by emphasizing four financial ratios which need to be considered at the onset of the examination process. The four help analysts and underwriters gather answers by focusing in on the business's overall trend and financial viability. The four ratios are as follows:

Profit Margin *(net income/sales).*

Current Ratio *(current assets/current liabilities).*

Total Asset Turnover *(total asset turnover (sales/total assets).*

Interest Coverage Ratio *(earnings before interest and taxes/interest expense).*

The ability to analyze financial statements is vitally important to the due diligence process; and may lead to the discovery of significant changes from prior periods. You will learn that findings of such incidents may warrant further investigation of the borrower's financial and tax transactions that could signal unpaid obligations or pending litigation. This analysis is first accomplished by the comparison of balance sheets and other financial statements through the use of financial ratios and other mathematical models.

These proven methods are significant in helping us look for earnings manipulations and in determining the overall financial health of the borrowing entity. It's equally important to know, these ratios assist the lender in determining the feasibility of the project and the ability of both to withstand the risks associated with the investment.

By the end of the book, you will have a better understanding of fraud in the commercial real estate process and will be enlightened at the lengths some people will go to misrepresent themselves just to steal your money. The purpose of the second edition is to bring awareness of the numerous fraud activities being committed and to increase your knowledge of the deterrence measures available that will aid in the due diligence process.

Chapter 1

Financial Due Diligence: Half the Battle is Knowing Where to Look

The dictionary defines due diligence as "the care that a reasonable person exercises to avoid harm to other persons or their property through performing research and analysis of a company or organization done to prepare for a business transaction."

Financial due diligence is just that. It's the process of an investigation conducted usually by a disinterested third party on behalf of a party contemplating a business transaction for the purpose of providing information with which to evaluate the advantages and risks involved. To be concise, the person conducting the due diligence is embarking on a "fact finding" mission, taking a neutral, unbiased position, sifting through documents, looking for information that's both in support and against another's position.

The Importance of Financial Due Diligence as it Relates to Commercial Real Estate

Having necessary and truthful information, removing the unknowns is fundamental in making sound business and investment decisions. In today's everchanging economic and political climate it's important to have all the facts when deciding to either buy a business, lend or invest in what is believed to be a sound commercial real estate project. Equally as important to the decision-making process is knowing that the other party has been truthful.

Those involved in commercial real estate know there will always be people who will misrepresent themselves, their intentions and often the property they're trying to sell, refinance or even develop. For our discussion, these same people to secure a deal may overstate both the projects' and their own; capabilities, assets, financials and performance. In addition, there may be an intentional failure to reveal pending bankruptcy, civil and sometimes past criminal actions.

Financial due diligence reduces risk by ensuring the credibility of all parties. Investors will conduct various forms of property due diligence to verify legal information and learn what they can about a property's past operating performance. While that's important, financial due diligence provides an extra check to ensure that all participants accurately present the subject property.

Forensic vs. Financial Audits

To better understand the need for financial due diligence, it is worthwhile to know the difference between a financial audit and a forensic audit. The financial audit usually conducted by a CPA is for the assurance that the borrower's financial statements, materially and fairly state the financial position as of a certain date. This audit is performed annually and can serve as a requirement for getting a loan. The forensic audit by definition is conducted periodically as a fraud prevention measure or if the borrower suspects an asset type theft. Money, materials, patented designs, etc.

Financial due diligence for commercial real estate, while concerned with the accuracy of the financial statements, is more interested in the truth behind the numbers presented. This is accomplished by means of a forensic audit in determining that both the financial statements and operational performance are as stated.

Financial due diligence... is accomplished by means of a forensic audit in determining that both the financial statements and operational performance are as stated.

5

Important! According to the ACFE's Report to the Nations on Occupational Fraud and Abuse in 2018, less than 4% of fraud is exposed by an external audit. Again, the purpose and objective of an external audit is for the auditor to express an opinion on the truth and fairness of the client's financial statements. The auditor accomplishes this by arbitrarily examining a select number of transactions during the audit. In fact, the auditor conducting such an audit is not charged with discovering asset-theft fraud.

Starting the process begins with the authorization to obtain information

In determining whether to extend a loan or loan commitment, the lender will review the books, records, financial statements and other information of the borrower and the commercial property during its due diligence process.

The lender and its representatives of a secured loan will conduct due diligence for two purposes:

- To determine if the borrower meets the lender's criteria
- Determine the appropriateness of the business terms governing the loan.

Due diligence for the first purpose is conducted by the lender. Due diligence for the second purpose ("legal" due diligence) is usually conducted by lender's counsel.

After the parties have agreed to proceed with the loan, the borrower will normally receive a request from the lender seeking further information related to the borrower and his/her business operations.

By law, the borrower must provide the lender with an "AUTHORIZATION TO OBTAIN AND RELEASE INFORMATION." Most often, it is the lender who prepares the release, and it is the borrower who signs the release and returns it to the lender.

The authorization to obtain information sent to the borrower by the lender may read something like this:

> I/We hereby authorize XYZ Bank to obtain any and all information they may require at any time for any purpose related to my/our credit transaction with XYZ Bank or any of its affiliated lenders, including obtaining my/our personal credit history from a consumer reporting agency, and I/we authorize the release of all such information to XYZ Bank or any of its affiliated lenders. I/We further authorize XYZ Bank to release such information to any entity they deem necessary for any purpose related to my/our credit transaction with them. I/We hereby certify that the enclosed information (plus any attachments or exhibits) is valid and correct to the best of my/our knowledge. I/We hereby acknowledge that all loan approvals will be in writing and subject to the terms and conditions set forth in a commitment letter signed by an officer of XYZ Bank or any of its affiliated lenders.

The following verbiage similar to offering a statement under penalty of perjury may be added to the authorization:

> All information provided to XYZ Bank is subject to the provisions of 18 U.S.C. §1001, which provides for civil and criminal penalties for a person that knowingly and willfully (1) falsifies or conceals a material fact; (2) makes any materially false or fraudulent statement or representation; or (3) makes or uses any false writing or document to XYZ Bank, whether in connection with an application or otherwise.

The Need for the Non-Disclosure Agreement

Following the request for confidential information regarding the borrower, it's business, its financials and its customers, the borrower should request that the lender execute a non-disclosure agreement (NDA) prior to beginning its due diligence.

A Non-Disclosure Agreement (NDA) is a legal document that protects any confidential information, and the nature of the discussions, from being disclosed to a third party. The agreement is designed to protect the confidentiality and free exchange of information in connection with the consideration and negotiation of the transaction during a party's due diligence review of the other. In effect, most transactions begin with an NDA. If there is any question of confidentiality or the importance of the information being shared, it is advisable to use an NDA.

The selling party may also request an NDA to be executed by the buyer prior to the disclosure of any documents or other confidential information about the sale or subsequent loan. This agreement protects both parties as in most cases, documents are disbursed via an online "data room" filled with loan documents and diligence materials (title, survey, environmental, financial statements, appraisals, etc.).

The NDA is designed to protect the confidentiality and free exchange of information.

Areas in Need of Examination/Due Diligence

Starting any financial due diligence process begins with the examination of the borrower's financial records. What "should happen" is that we find the information in these records to be the same as what's been reported elsewhere. For example, the expenses reported on the Profit and Loss statement should match the Schedule C or 1120S of the borrower's federal income tax filing. The Borrower's existing loans should be shown as liabilities on the borrower's balance sheet, etc. If not, we need to ask why?

From the lender's request for information of the borrower, the following items at a minimum should be available for examination:

Signed Financial Statements from Borrowers and Guarantors to Include:

- Annual and Quarterly Financial Information for the Past Three years
- Balance Sheets
- Profit and Loss Statements
- Statement of Cash Flows
- Rent Rolls
- Audit Results for the Past Five Years
- Tax Returns for the Past Three Years
- Borrower's Income Projections
- Liabilities to Include Existing Loans
- UCC Records
- Capital Structure
- Legal and Related Matters
- Project / Financial Projections
- Project / Market Analysis

Other Items that are part of the Due Diligence Process Include:

- Evidence that property taxes are not in arrears
- Property pledged as collateral have Parcel Identification Numbers to include legal description and are not subject to a Parcel split.
- Phase I Environmental Report that is current and does not state that further action or review is warranted.

Financial Due Diligence Includes the Request and Examination of these Records

Required are annual and quarterly financial information for the past three years to see if the business is trending upward, downward or if significant changes have occurred during the past three reporting periods.

Reviewing the audit results for the past five years is a great indicator of the borrower's company operations. Questions to ask include:

- What recommendations did the auditors make?
- Did the company comply with the recommendations?
- Was the auditing firm the same as in previous years or was it recently changed, leaving one to question why?

Tax returns for the past three years are indicators that the borrower is:

- Filing his tax returns, and
- Does the information from Schedule C concur with the company's profit-and-loss statements?

Balance sheets are useful for comparison when looking for variances or changes in the composition of a specific group of accounts. In addition, the examination of the borrower's balance sheet is needed for analysis when determining if fraud had occurred. One area that should not be overlooked is the company's inventory. Ask questions!

- When was the last time a physical and/or periodic count of the inventory was conducted?
- How much of the inventory was found to be obsolete?
- Is the valuation accurate?

Accounts Receivable needs to be examined to ensure "lapping" (stealing from deposits) has not occurred which is accomplished by checking to see if the company has consistently reconciled its bank statements with the company's ledger.

- Do deposits match what has been posted?

This reconciliation procedure is best performed by someone other than the person making the deposits.

We examine accounts payable in most cases to detect disbursement fraud. Questions to ask include:

- Are the vendors real?
- Have they have made multiple payments?
- Are the invoiced figures in rounded amounts or are the amounts billed/requested just below the level of approval?

Profit and loss statements should be examined to determine if numbers have been changed. The lower the reported expenses, the higher the net income will be for the same period. Another method used by fraudsters called "Improper Timing" is to delay the reporting of certain expenses to a later period. This in turn, raises the net income for the current period higher than what should have been reported.

False asset values on an income statement will appear as a negative cash flow, yet growth in earnings could mean that manipulation or over-valuing the fair market value of assets has occurred. If the depreciation methods used do not conform to those recognized by GAAP or standard accounting procedures, an overstatement of the assets' life will decrease the reported depreciation expense. All that means is the asset that has a prescribed depreciation period has not correctly been depreciated. So, the asset shows on the balance sheet of greater than actual value while the depreciation expense account is lower than what should've been reported.

Another method called "Improper Timing" involves not reporting certain expenses for the period which raises the income figures.

Borrower's income projections need to make sense.

- Have they increased the income projections hoping to receive a larger loan commitment?
- What is the trend compared to previous reporting periods?

- Besides current operations, are new products or services forecasted or being offered at a later date?

Liabilities to include existing loans is finding out what the borrower really owes.

- What is the ratio of liabilities to assets?
- Has the total amount of liabilities increased in the past several periods?
- Is the company borrowing money to stay afloat?

A question that needs asking: Have the income projections been increased with the expectation of receiving a larger loan commitment?

UCC records (Uniform Commercial Code-1) is a legal form that a creditor files to give notice that it has or may have an interest in the personal property (or equipment) of a debtor. This is especially important if the seller reports various assets as "paid in full" or misrepresents leased assets as "owned" assets. UCC records need to be examined to determine if a loan exists against an asset that may be incorrectly listed on the balance sheet.

Capital structure is how a company finances its overall operations and growth by using different sources of funds. Debt comes in the form of bond issues or long-term notes payable, while equity is classified as common stock, preferred stock, or retained earnings.

Is the borrower raising capital by securing loans or is he offering an equity position to investors through the issuance of stock. Convertible preferred stock which begins as debt offers the holder the option to convert the debt into equity shares at a later date.

Legal and related matters such as liens, judgments, encumbrances and Lis pendens need to be examined. Judgments, encumbrances and liens against the sellers or borrower's property can be found on the preliminary title report. A Lis pendens is a notice recorded with the county recorder's office stating that the right of ownership or possession of a piece of real estate is the subject of an existing lawsuit. Also note. Be aware of federal (IRS) tax liens and judgments from others listed on the property title report. All of which may need to be satisfied if the borrower needs financing to complete the sale.

Project/financial projections are numbers provided through feasibility studies or by information provided to the buyer from the seller. For the commercial real estate buyer, it has always been imperative to fully examine all lease agreements, estoppels, approved uses, taxes and property conditions.

- Does the pro forma fairly represent the expected revenues, expenses and overall costs (to include financing costs)?
- Does the proforma accurately represent what is needed to operate and maintain the real estate?
- For an existing project, are historical costs used as a baseline for measuring the projected costs?
- If not, what footnotes or explanations are given for the differences?

Project/market analysis much like a SWOT analysis is studying certain characteristics and trends of a market to determine its strengths, weaknesses, opportunities, and threats. A commercial real estate developer in determining the feasibility of a retail project development would likely include reported numbers from the surrounding area to include: retail occupancy/vacancy rates, current rents, projected rental rates, and trends.

Complete market analysis of these rates and trends would likely include those of neighboring commercial real estate properties offering comparable amenities, demographic or population trends, schools, safety and law enforcement, shopping and banking, methods of transportation, municipal or county governance, zoning ordinances, traffic counts and patterns.

Borrowers and Third-Party Licenses

When learning the borrower intends to manufacture a product in which another holds a patent, make it a priority to actually view the third-party license. It was during one of my first assignments where I learned a valuable lesson.

Reading through the business plan, I learned the borrower sought to borrow more than $30 million dollars. It was during the first trip I learned the borrower was purchasing an industrial building and a monthly option was being paid to keep the sale alive.

Prior to the assignment, it was my understanding that the investor had reviewed the loan request submitted by the borrower and wanted clarification on several points. The due diligence they asked me to perform centered on a borrower looking to manufacture a new product. In addition, the status of the guarantor was unclear.

Yet, it was a month after the first visit when I discovered the borrowing entity did not have the legal right to manufacture the product in which they intended to market. At the time of the loan request, and unbeknownst to the lender, the patent holder on the east coast had not reached an agreement with the borrower and withheld a third-party license.

It was on a subsequent trip to the patent holder's east coast location that I learned of this and realized there was no agreement between the patent holder and the borrower. Besides learning the license to manufacture would not happen any time soon; it was the comments made by the borrower that the guaranteeing entity was "sketchy" which prompted me to offer a less than favorable opinion of the borrower.

Lesson learned: Information regarding the third-party license had not been disclosed upfront, but it was my responsibility to find out, and I should've asked. With borrowers engaged in manufacturing, don't be timid. Ask to see if third-party licenses are an issue and if so, do they exist?

Fraud Related Internal Controls

When examining the borrower's accounting records, be alert to questionable or suspicious activity. Though not all that appears to be fraud is. However, a person committing fraudulent acts will often leave a trail or indicators characteristic of their suspect activity. In cases like this, it is recommended the examiner report their findings to the client.

Violations of internal controls relating to financial reporting usually fall into one of the five categories listed below:

<u>Fictitious Revenue Schemes</u> occur when a company, for example, alters an invoice upwards, records sales that do not exist or reports sales to a fictitious customer to show a higher than existing level of revenue.

<u>Improper Timing Schemes</u> occur when legitimate revenues or expenses are posted in later accounting periods to meet existing budgets, forecasts or financial goals. The result is the net income for the period is "overstated" while the expenses are "understated" and have been postponed to the next accounting period where they will then be posted.

Understating Liabilities and Expenses (falsely) inflates the net income, resulting in overstating the owner's equity.

This can also happen when expenses are not recorded. A second way is to capitalize expenses (and amortize them) increasing both income and assets instead of being expensed immediately. Third, examine the account, "Returns and Allowances" for accuracy as several products sold are often returned as defective or other reasons. One way to find out is to compare this figure as a percentage to previous periods. Are they consistent? It is management's duty to estimate the amount and make provisions for it.

<u>Improper Disclosure Schemes</u> include failing to disclose important notes or misleading comments on financial statements. This includes the failure to attach narratives, supporting schedules, loan covenants or contingencies, related party transactions, management fraud or even changes in accounting policies, all of which can result in misleading potential investors as to the true financial condition of the company.

Improper Asset Valuation Schemes include the fraudulent "overstatement" of inventory or receivables giving the appearance that the borrower has more assets then what's actually on hand. That's why periodic inventories are necessary.

A person committing fraudulent acts will often leave a trail.

Red Flags

Red Flags are warning signs, identifying those activities that give rise to further examination. A red flag can be behavioral or an action that raises concern. During the course of conducting financial due diligence, it's highly recommended that the topics listed below are addressed. The answers found will help in forming an opinion as to the character of the borrower's operation.

Red Flags to be on the Lookout for Include:

- Delinquent Real Estate Taxes
- Declining Sales Prices or Rental Rates
- Cancellations in Sales Contracts or Reservations
- Liberal Concessions to Include Free Rent, Moving Allowances, Tenant Improvement Allowances, etc.
- Slower Absorption or Rent Up of Space in New Projects
- Delinquent Lease Payments from Major or Anchor Tenants
- Upward Trending Higher Vacancy and Turnover Rates

What do company records show?

Altered Documents: Discovering altered inventory records, shipping documents, appraisals, valuation reports or contracts with dates that appear to have been changed are all definitely "red flags" and deserve proper explanations.

Multiple Records: In a limited number of cases, especially those involving taxes, one may find a legitimate second set of records. However, schemes involving both a manufactured and a maintained set of accounting records would be a strong indicator of fraud. An example of which would be two sets of accounts receivable. The question then is, "How much is the company really owed?"

Destruction of Records: The first thing that comes to mind is..."It must be fraud"! However, most reputable companies have policies with an established timetable for the shredding of documents held beyond the required hold period. It is when the timing of such destruction becomes suspicious. As an example, upon the announcement of an impending audit, lawsuit or investigation, it's learned documents related to the matter are being destroyed. That can and probably is illegal and should be considered a red flag!

Finding the Right Person to Talk to

Interviews are great tool for understanding the internal workings of a company and who is responsible for doing what. These interviews include speaking confidentially with members of management and to staff at all levels. Interviews often paint a picture of the culture and what's it like to work there? In the beginning stages of the due diligence process or even during a fraud assessment, it is important to determine if an employee has seen or experienced any activity that appears questionable. Keep in mind, a higher than average rate of employee turnover is an issue. It's always good to find out what the average length of employment is, and are workers satisfied? Websites like www.glassdoor.com and www.indeed.com often provide company reviews from past and current employees.

Find out from employees the true story of what's going on with the borrower.

Let me begin by saying that it's vitally important for members of management to properly set the tone regarding fraud prevention. This means the internal controls that were created and meant to be followed by employees are in fact, not being circumvented by those occupying positions in top management. Ask yourself, what lender would want to do business with a company where management doesn't enforce a policy of internal controls that they themselves had created? If members of management can't keep their own hands out of the cookie jar, then possibly a bigger problem exists.

In writing a business plan for a foreign manufacturer, an important piece of information was revealed during the interview. The son of one of the partners was provided access to huge sums of money that he later used for investing in real estate. I'm not implying this young man was not qualified, but I am saying members of the executive team should've exercised greater oversight and had said no! In fact, the investments later turned into significant losses.

For many, investing in real estate or any other industry that is believed to be trending downward can be a scary thought. In this case, the son of a company executive, one of questionable experience, invested several hundred thousand dollars of corporate earnings towards the purchase of speculative real estate. Wait a minute, the core product of this manufacturer was to produce paint.

The result is that over $500,000 in US dollars was lost during a two-year period. The amount subsequently affected the company's cash position and impeded its ability to operate.

To learn more about a potential borrower, my suggestion would be to speak with someone from accounting and others from the shipping department.

Vendor Complaints: If possible, talk to vendors and ask about their experiences with the borrower. Is the borrower described as a "slow pay?" and second, what has been the success rate when bidding on the borrower's projects?

If possible, talk to vendors and ask about their experiences.

Chapter 2

Lenders and Risk Management

In pursuit of increasing one's knowledge in the area of financial due diligence, this chapter addresses the various risks and legislation facing both traditional banks and non-bank lenders.

We begin the chapter by addressing the 5 C's of Credit used by lenders in evaluating loan applicants, followed by analyzing the "Borrower and Guarantor's Financial Condition;" the "Loans Secured by Owner-Occupied Properties" and "Evaluating Guarantees." Next, the areas to be discussed include the differences between recourse and non-recourse Loans, The Patriot Act and Dodd-Frank. What each of these are and how they affect traditional banks and non-bank lenders.

The 5 C's of Credit

Let's refresh our memory with a discussion of the 5 C's of credit. Banks subject to federal legislation and those not are both likely to subscribe to the five C's of credit when determining whom to loan to and the amount available to lend. The five C's are character, capital, capacity, conditions, and collateral. Banks use this method to gain a better understanding of the borrower and to mitigate the risk of default on a loan. They are detailed as follows:

Character

Lenders look closely at the character of its loan applicants in determining a willingness and ability to repay. Indicators such as bankruptcy filings, credit score and borrowing history besides factors such as honesty and integrity are examined in determining whether or not to make the loan. The last two are usually found by exploring the borrower's change in residences, criminal and employment history.

Capital

Knowledge of the borrower's capital position assists the bank to better understand the prospective borrower's business and personal wealth. The greater the amount of capital, the more likely the borrower can tolerate times of difficulty and volatility. A strong capital position can also represent the commitment an owner or borrowing entity maintains, which provides reassurance to the lender of the borrower's capacity to repay the loan.

Capacity

Underwriters look to the capacity of the borrower to repay a loan. We define capacity as the borrower's ability to generate the cash flow necessary to service the principal and interest on a loan. A strong cash flow from normalized business activities demonstrates the borrower's ability to repay the debt and provides the lender with assurance of the reduced probability of default. Determining capacity makes it necessary for the lender to examine three or more years of financial statements in order to establish a trend in the borrower's business operations.

A strong capital position can represent the borrowing entity's commitment... (which) provides reassurance to the lender of the borrower's capacity to repay the loan.

Conditions

A major question that deserves an answer is; "What are the current and projected conditions affecting the borrower and his business in an ever-changing economy?"

We know that a surge in (industry) growth and a strong economy will support a business's ability to generate cash and repay any debt. What about if there was a slowdown? Is the borrower engaged in an industry that's market-sensitive? Will the borrower be able to meet his financial obligations? This is exactly why an understanding of current economic trends is critical in analyzing the borrower's position.

Collateral

Lenders will in most cases place a lien on the borrower's other property as collateral. In the event of default, a lender may have to rely on the quality and marketability of this other property in an effort to satisfy the loan. A critical analysis of the pledged collateral supporting a loan is an important step before the actual granting of a loan.

What is the status and quality of the borrower's other assets to include; real estate, equipment, and inventory?

The Case of the Mixed-Use Property on Wilshire Blvd.

While the construction lender will focus on the project's future potential, the typical commercial real estate property lender will place greater emphasis on the income produced by the existing property. Described below is the "exception to the rule."

A client of mine, I'll call Gus asked me to call his cousin, Marvin. Gus's cousin owned a two-story mixed-use building with ample parking and wanted to refinance in order to draw out $1,000,000 in cash. Pictures were taken and the loan worksheet was prepared and submitted to the underwriting department in order to receive from them a Letter of Intent (LOI). A few days later came the response. The answer was No. An immediate call was then placed to the area manager who took my side and could not understand underwriting's reasoning and asked them to reconsider.

The property:

Marvin's small two-story mixed-use office over retail property was located along Wilshire Boulevard deep in the heart of Santa Monica. An upscale 2 Cap area. The single acre, a corner lot by itself, was worth upwards of $4 million dollars.

Since our bank made loans that were not subordinate to others, this was a win-win situation for both the borrower and the bank. Even the worst-case scenario had the bank taking claim to a $4 million lot plus an income-producing building if the borrower could not make the payments. The underwriting department located 50 miles away finally understood what was at hand and granted the loan. This case was definitely an exception to the rule!

Analysis of Borrower and Guarantor's Financial Condition

Banks and the Borrower

The bank's priority and fiduciary responsibility is to institute and maintain credit underwriting guidelines that provide for both scrutiny and proper analysis before issuing a credit commitment.

This practice takes into account the following:

- Borrower's overall financial condition
- Resources and responsibility of the guarantor
- Nature and value of the collateral being offered
- Borrower's character and willingness to repay as agreed.

To meet the guidelines established by the credit committee, the bank will need to get the appropriate financial information on the borrower(s) and guarantor(s), thus answering questions of income, liquidity, cash flow, contingent liabilities, and other relevant factors.

Through the underwriting process, a decision will ultimately be made as to the borrower's capacity to meet a realistic repayment plan from his/her available liquidity and cash flow. Cash flow or revenue generated from the underlying property besides other indicators of the borrower's capacity should be evaluated to determine if the borrower can adequately and consistently through the life of the loan service both the interest and principal on a prospective loan.

Many banks subscribe to the belief that cash flows should be assessed on a global basis. Global cash-flow analysis means evaluating the borrower's entire financial condition. This would include examining the borrower's multiple sources of income (if more than one), and cash flows from business financial statements, tax returns and Schedule K-1 forms for multiple partnerships, limited liability companies (LLCs) and corporations. The analysis takes into account all required and discretionary cash flows from the borrower's activities giving special attention to contingent liabilities and their potential effect on the borrower's capacity to repay the proposed loan amount.

Where the borrower or business has relied substantially or depends on capital gains for its source of income, the focus of the analysis will center on recurring cash flows and expected capital gains. Projections of expenses such as personal debt payments, property and income taxes, and living expenses should also be considered.

Be prepared as banks will often review financial statements from the past three years to establish a trend line to gain a better understanding of the borrower's practices. Significant liquid assets or short-term instruments including cash, stocks, bonds, and annuities will be included in the bank's analysis, as these assets may be called upon to fund other actual or contingent liabilities or cash flow shortfalls.

Be aware, there will be situations where lenders place a greater emphasis on the quality of the property, its location and the strength of the borrower instead of asking for tax returns.

Banks and non-bank lenders will often review the past three years of financial statements to establish a trend line to gain a better understanding of the borrower's practices.

The Guarantor

Before the bank accepts the guarantor, questions that deserves answers are, "Does the guarantor know the difference between a co-signer and a guarantor?" "Do they understand the guarantor has have no legal claim to the property?" In contrast, the co-signer is a co-owner of the asset. "Does the person acting as the guarantor have the willingness and capacity to provide support, and do they understand that the guarantee is legally enforceable?"

23

Presuming a willingness to provide support to the borrower (or project) exists, the lender needs to determine the guarantor's economic incentive to do so? The guarantor should be advised to seek legal counsel before agreeing to move forward. Bank analysts must determine whether a guarantor has shown in the past a willingness to fulfill prior commitments or obligations. Is the economic incentive provided to the guarantor appropriate and sufficient? Finally, does the guarantor have a significant interest and are they financially invested in the project?

The Lender may also consider the guarantor's global financial condition such as their: income, liquidity, cash flow, contingent liabilities, and other relevant factors (including a satisfactory credit rating) to show the guarantor's financial capacity to fulfill the obligation. This assessment of the guarantor should include the total number and amount of guarantees currently extended and whether the guarantor has the financial wherewithal to fulfill the contingent claims that may already exist.

Besides determining the global financial condition of the guarantor, the lender will take into consideration the liquidity of the guarantor's assets that have been called upon or pledged to collateralize the guarantee.

Note to self: Guarantees may be limited in nature, such as interest-only, construction completion only, partial principal, stepped-down in amount, or even released during the loan term as certain conditions are met.

Throughout the repayment period, the bank will monitor and assess the borrower's performance toward satisfying the loan conditions before releasing a guarantor of their obligation. The lender in most instances through the addition of covenants added to the loan documents will require the borrower to submit periodically usually quarterly, financial information which allows the lender to sufficiently monitor and track the financial soundness of both the borrower and guarantor.

The assessment of the guarantor should include the total number and amount of guarantees currently extended.

Evaluating Guarantees

A guarantee offered from a responsible guarantor with a proven track record often improves the prospects for repayment of the debt obligation. In many cases, lenders will lessen or reduce the risk classification. Simply, the better the financial condition of the guarantor, the less risk is placed on the lender, and the more likely the borrower will receive a favorable interest rate when being considered for a loan.

Lenders when analyzing the guarantee, look for:

- The financial capacity and willingness of the guarantor to provide credit support through ongoing payments, curtailments or re-margining.
- The agreed-upon guarantee is legally enforceable and is adequate to provide support for repayment of the indebtedness, in whole or in part, during the remaining loan term.

The better the financial condition of the guarantor, the less risk placed on the lender, and the more likely the borrower will receive a favorable interest rate...

Bad Boy Guaranty

Carve out provisions, aka a "bad boy guaranty," protects the lender by allowing personal recourse with the occurrence of certain events, such as fraud or bankruptcy. Essentially, bad boy guarantees are exceptions to the non-recourse status of a loan which prevent the borrower from siphoning cash from the property in the months leading up to a loan default. The guarantee varies by state, but here are some common carve out provisions of bad boy clauses included in non-recourse loans:

- Filing for bankruptcy
- Fraud or misrepresentation
- Failure to maintain required insurance
- Failure to pay property taxes
- Any environmental indemnification
- Committing a criminal act

The bad boy guaranty is not limited to the above major events or bad acts and has been expanded to include more and more minor provisions, such as the failure to deliver financial statements to the lender as agreed or the failure of the borrower to permit lender inspections of the property. Terms of the bad boy guarantee can vary from state to state leaving these and other minor carve out provisions left up to state lawmakers.

Analyzing Repayment Capacity of the Borrower/Property

The underwriter's primary task when reviewing a commercial loan application and binding commitments is determining the borrower's ability to repay the loan. Points of focus being considered include:

- The borrower's willingness and capacity to repay the loan under reasonable terms.
- The cash flow potential of the underlying collateral or business.

In the course of the review, underwriters will also factor in:

- The Borrower's character, overall financial condition, resources, and payment record. The nature and level of protection provided by the cash flow from business operations or the collateral if on a global basis when considering the borrower's total debt obligations.
- Market conditions that could influence the prospects of repayment and cash flow potential from the borrower's business operations or underlying collateral.
- Prospects for repayment support from any financially responsible guarantors.

Loans Secured by Owner-Occupied Properties

The primary source of repayment from owner-occupied properties is usually the cash flow generated by the borrower's occupying business. Lenders for the most part will consider the ability of all three: the occupying business, the borrower, and guarantors in the debt's repayment.

Lender Risk Management

There are several risks associated with commercial real estate lending. Of a possible eight, there are four we need to know in the course of our financial due diligence. They are:

- Credit Risk
- Interest Rate Risk
- Liquidity Risk
- Operational Risk

Additional risks not included in the list that are discussed include:

- Environmental risk
- Market risk

Credit Risk

Credit risk is the risk taken by the lender at the time they make a loan. The risk is later realized when it becomes apparent the borrower will fail to meet its obligations in accordance with agreed terms. A subsequent default on the loan can occur should the borrower fail to cure the loan. The risk to the lender (when quantified) as a total can include loss of principal and interest, disruption to cash flows, and increased collection costs.

As one can see, the financial condition of the borrower and the current value of any underlying collateral significantly affects the lender's interest. Again, the leading goal of the credit risk department is to maximize a lender's risk-adjusted rate of return by maintaining its credit risk exposure to within acceptable parameters.

Interest Rate Risk

Interest rate risk refers to future unknown changes in earnings within a commercial lending portfolio resulting from interest rate movement, primarily short-term interest rates such as the LIBOR or prime rate. The lender dependent upon the makeup of his or her portfolio mix can limit or mitigate the exposure in several ways: 1.)requiring a higher DSCR, 2.)offering a lower loan to value (LTV), 3.)increasing the spread on fixed-rate loans, 4.)offering variable rate loan products or a combination of both. Example of which may be a loan product requiring a higher DSCR, lower LTV on a 10-year loan with a fixed rate for 5 or fewer years at 2.5 pts above the Prime rate followed by a floating variable rate (reset every 6 months) for the final years of the loan term and 5.)The lender could reduce the amortization period from 30 to 25 years to collect a greater amount of principal and interest during the first years.

Liquidity Risk

A third risk facing lenders is that of liquidity risk, which can be described as the risk of a funding crisis. In other words, the lender may not have the funds available to meet the market demand for loans.

Risk management is all about managing the liquidity and portfolio structure. With today's heightened regulations and scrutiny on product type concentration, many bank lenders are selling even their performing commercial real estate loans to decrease the dollar amount and/or CRE concentrations (loan types) being held in their lending portfolio. Secondary market sales have become more the norm, which has markedly helped make the sale of CRE loans more acceptable.

In periods where the real estate market or even the economy is experiencing difficulty, CRE loans can become less liquid. The effect of having a reduction in tenants often leads to office or even retail properties becoming less liquid compared to those of multifamily or owner-occupied properties. Sources of funding can all but disappear, leaving lenders to allocate fewer funds for real estate investments. This in effect, forces lenders to offer fewer new loans and can sometimes limit their ability to refinance existing ones.

Operational Risk

While operational risk exists in all products and services, commercial real estate lending, particularly "Acquisition, Development and Construction (ADC) loans," present a greater operational risk than other types of lending. Before providing a loan, lenders will often require developers to line up tenants willing to lease once space becomes available.

The second part to lessen the effects of operational risk is for lenders to address the risk head-on. Lenders need competent and practical systems in place in order to properly monitor property performance to include the borrower being required to submit quarterly financial statements on the real estate and pledged collateral. Regarding construction or ADC loans, effective monitoring and disbursement of loan proceeds and repayment can control progress.

Lenders must have a plan to protect their interests in the collateral by ensuring that property taxes, insurance premiums, workers, and suppliers are being paid.

Lenders will often require developers to line up tenants that are willing to lease once space becomes available.

Environmental risk

Contamination that can occur from businesses like gas stations, plating operations and dry cleaners may negatively affect the value of the real property or collateral by exposing the lender to unnecessary liability arising from violations of various environmental laws. Therefore, the lender will in most cases require a Phase I environmental report to assess the potential adverse effect of environmental contamination. This is a common requirement (loan condition) prior to the bank or private lender being associated with the real estate or the property that has been taken as collateral.

Side Note

Several years ago, while working at the bank, a loan request was brought to me from a local broker representing a client desiring to refinance a retail property in an upscale area of Los Angeles. The broker made the claim and signed the document stating that to the best of his knowledge, no environmentally adverse activity had taken place on that property. Low and behold, the Phase I Environmental Report came back citing that over 50 years earlier, a gas station had been in operation at that location. While someone had removed the tanks, no member of the Fire department had submitted a report relating to their removal so the comment "Further investigation is warranted" was stated on the bottom of the opening page of the Phase I Environmental Report.

Luckily, for the borrower, the fuel storage tanks had not been located below the current two-story structure; Rather, the tanks had been in the ground below the adjacent parking area. $5,000, a few months and several tests later, the property received a clean bill of health and the bank subsequently made the loan. Lessons learned here; even brokers can be wrong and the lender was correct in ordering a Phase I report and requiring the subsequent clean-up.

Environmental Liability and the Law

Exemptions to the law such as "not participating in the management of the business" do not limit the lender's liability for cleanup. These exemptions also do not protect the lender from the decline in value that contamination can cause during the remediation process.

It is the lender who should perform an evaluation of the borrower's or tenant's business activities and any property taken as collateral **before** funding a loan and before taking title in satisfaction of debt.

In addition, the same exemptions do not protect a responsible borrower from the liability. Keep in mind, the cost of cleanup or remediation can severely impair the borrower's ability to repay the loan.

Market risk

We know for a fact the real estate industry is susceptible to cyclical highs and lows. While strong markets are often characterized by low vacancy rates and steady growth, market downturns often result in a lower number of occupancies and sometimes discounted or periods of free rent. There are several factors that can prompt a lopsidedness or imbalance in the supply and demand for space.

For example, we know the departure of a town's only factory employing hundreds of people will have an adverse effect on home ownership and real estate prices. On the other hand, a booming economy may lead to a surge in hotel development resulting in an oversupply of rooms causing innkeepers to drop room rates to maintain a competitive edge. Market risk can often be projected months in advance and mitigated through proper planning.

Types of Loans - Recourse and Non-Recourse Loans

In a recourse loan, the borrower or guarantors are personally liable for repaying any outstanding balance on the loan, besides the collateral itself. If the collateral securing a loan needs to be liquidated but remains insufficient to cover the total amount owed, then "recourse" enables the lender to go after the guarantors personally to cover any deficiency. Full recourse loans are common with construction and other shorter-term commercial real estate financing, such as a mini-perm loan that finances lease-up and stabilization of an asset. The mini-perm is commonly used to pay off a construction loan and fills in the gap until attractive longer-term funding can be secured.

Non-Recourse

A non-recourse loan is where both the borrower and/or guarantors are NOT personally liable for repaying any of the outstanding balance on the loan. Non-recourse financing is typically found on longer-term permanent commercial real estate loans placed on a stabilized and performing asset such as multifamily apartments.

However, the common misconception with non-recourse loans is that a borrower or guarantor can never be held personally liable in the case of default. While on the surface the concept sounds good, the fact is borrowers pay a higher interest rate and several exemptions to the rule called "carve-out provisions" or the "bad boy guaranty" exist.

Patriot Act and Commercial Real Estate

The Patriot Act has two sections, of which 326 and 352 apply directly to commercial lending. Section 326 requires banks and lenders to know their client through verification, while section 352 relates to lenders taking steps to curb anti-money laundering activities.

Section 326: Customer Identification Verification requires all financial institutions to implement procedures to verify the identity of customers at the time an account is opened. The Patriot Act requires financial institutions to implement procedures beyond that of verification by (a) maintaining the records of the information used to verify the person's identity; and (b) consulting with "lists of known or suspected terrorists or terrorist organizations provided to the financial institution by any government agency" and to determine if any customer is included on such a list.

Section 352: addresses money laundering by requiring each "financial institution" to establish anti-money laundering programs. These programs need to include, at a minimum:

- The development of internal anti-money laundering procedures, policies, and controls designed to detect and prevent money laundering, this includes a "Know Your Customer" program designed to identify prospective customers/clients and the source of their assets.

- The designation of an internal compliance officer.

- The same institution is responsible for the development of an ongoing employee training program covering: applicable legal requirements, policies and procedures for monitoring client relationships, acceptable record-keeping measures, and the

32

identification of suspicious transactions or money laundering activities.

- Finally, the financial institution must develop and implement an independent audit function to test and review the company's due diligence programs.

Foreign Investors/Borrowers

The term "foreign national" includes someone that was not born in the U.S. but has subsequently moved here and has met the requirements to obtain a "Green Card." The Green Card is yet another name for a "permanent resident visa." The visa allows the holder to stay in the U.S. indefinitely (if they continue to meet the continuous residency requirements) affording them most of the privileges of a full citizen with the exception they cannot vote in a public election.

Green Card holders who are permanent residents, possessing a social security number, a U.S. bank account and credit history from one or more of the credit rating bureaus will find that it is not very difficult to obtain real estate funding or the ability to refinance a real estate loan. The cardholder may have to provide certain forms relating to income and or payment of various sales taxes. The lender still has certain special requirements (under the Patriot Act) to check certain lists to make sure their loan applicant is not a "terrorist." Above that, the permanent resident of the U.S. will not face difficulties over and above that of a U.S. citizen.

The same cannot be said for a foreign national that does not possess a Green Card. For example, the foreign investor wanting to buy real estate here in the United States will find it nearly impossible to locate a traditional lender that will make them a commercial loan.

Hard money lenders with fewer restrictions may assist while traditional lenders will most likely require several years of tax returns, credit reports, not to mention a credit score from a major credit reporting bureau. In addition, lenders will most likely expect the foreign borrower to have conducted a substantial amount of business in the United States.

In most cases, traditional lenders will ask for a guarantor. That is someone with substantial financial assets who will step in and guarantee the loan. If the market goes south and the real estate declines in value, the bank may secure a judgment against the personal guarantor of the loan. Be prepared for the possibility the commercial lender will require any individual with more than a 10% ownership interest in the borrowing entity to be a guarantor for the commercial loan.

The foreign borrower is expected to have conducted a substantial amount of business in the United States.

Lenders and the Development of Commercial Properties Outside the United States

While writing a business plan for a large-scale residential project in Ulaanbaatar Mongolia, the issue of property ownership was raised by the lender. At the time, under Mongolian law, a foreign national was restricted and could only purchase a "land use" permit. Apparently, the Korean-owned developer/construction company working in partnership with the Mongolian national was not enough to satisfy the Korean based lender.

As of August 2016, Mongolian citizens could own real estate. However, difficulties still existed for corporate entities of any type, foreign or domestic, from owning real estate. While foreigners and foreign firms may own the structures outright, the parcel of land they occupy can only be obtained through the leasing of land use rights. Terms of the leases range from one (1) to ninety (90) years.

In China, the ownership of real estate and land usage rights have been separate issues as China practices 'socialist public' ownership of all land. As in the case of Mongolia, obtaining land usage rights in China allows the property owner (leaseholder) to manage the land to develop houses and buildings or even pledge them as collateral. However, true ownership of the land continues to belong to the state, which also maintains the right to withdraw the land leasing rights mid-term.

The purpose of the above examples while the information is believed to be correct, provide the reader with an understanding of the difficulties a developer or foreign lender may encounter.

For reference, a list of countries that appear favorable to foreign development and ownership is provided. Please keep in mind that the list is not complete, and the countries listed and their terms of property ownership are subject to change. Developers are encouraged to research land purchase/ownership rights of each country they plan to develop within.

Countries with Few or No Restrictions

- United Kingdom
- France
- New Zealand
- Spain
- Tahiti
- Italy
- Canada
- Fiji
- Brazil
- Bahamas
- Australia
- Argentina

Countries with Some Restrictions

- Mexico
- Costa Rica

Countries that can be Difficult or Adverse to Foreign-Owned Development

- Thailand
- China
- Mongolia

- Vietnam
- Cuba

Non-Bank aka Private Lenders: An Option Worth Exploring

Non-Bank or Private Lenders

This shift in lending to nonbanks and private lenders is largely attributed to an overwhelming number of traditional banks and their aversion to risk. At one time, private lenders found it difficult competing head to head with traditional banks (on A-paper loans) and were relegated to lending to borrowers with credit issues including tax liens and judgments. Today, these same non-bank, private lenders are being viewed as a credible lending source for funding most types of commercial real estate transactions ranging from simple refinancing of stabilized multifamily properties to large construction projects.

While traditional banks for years have focused on lower-risk construction projects by well-known entities, private lenders looking to fill the void have seized the opportunity by their willingness to fund developers and projects most traditional lenders would've passed on. Yes, the transactions involve more risk than traditional banks wish to undertake. However, developers having projects that fall outside of the strict lending parameters of traditional banks have found interested funding sources through these nonbank lenders.

Private lenders are no longer viewed as the dubious hard money lenders of years past, when the term private money had a negative connotation. Some nonbank private lenders of today control billions of dollars of funds that are immediately available for investment. Many of these same lenders now reside in high rise office towers with their MBA's and are often called upon to finance large-scale projects well into the nine-figure range. As lending requirements tightened, leaving fewer borrowers able to meet the strict standards, traditional banks have all but found their once-thriving lending practices downsized or even eliminated. The once frowned upon private lenders now find themselves extremely active funding loans of significant size.

Private lenders... have seized the opportunity by their willingness to fund developers and projects that traditional lenders would've passed on.

Smaller Non-Bank Lenders

Besides the fact that specialty non-bank lenders are funding large projects, there are still smaller nonbank sources that will fund whatever remaining costs of a project as long as a significant amount of funding has already been invested by the principals. Terms can vary from lender to lender, and the major deciding factor can be the industry, the project, or the amount already invested in the project.

Keep in mind, high-LTV lenders are still out there offering low fees and minimal due-diligence costs. To find them, one just has to look online. Many of these lenders use due-diligence processes and valuation activities conducted entirely by third-parties who specialize in providing the same services for the world's largest financial institutions. These companies will usually contract with the client directly and send a report to the lender upon completion of the assignment.

In Pursuit of the Best ROI

Nonbank sources of funds frequently include organizations like pension funds, investment banks, insurance companies, endowments, family offices, and even some commercial banks. The funds they have at their disposal are usually substantial and readily available, which positions many private lenders to finance large-scale projects. The increasing involvement from these nonbank sources result from the need to actively seek suitable projects to invest in so they can meet the objectives of their institutional investors who desire an adequate return on their investment.

Many nonbanks have large amounts of capital available, which allows them in most cases to offer rates and terms comparable to that of your more traditional (often familiar) banks. These private lenders can fund riskier projects that do not qualify for traditional bank financing but yield higher returns. As a result, these lenders have become more attractive to institutional investors replacing the need for a massive number of small individual investors as their primary source of capital.

These sophisticated investors (namely the financial institutions) are the ones nonbank lenders cannot afford to lose by making bad loan decisions. Again, nonbank lenders have a single aim in their business, which is to produce sufficient or exceptional returns for their investors.

Lending Requirements on Par with Banks

The risk-management techniques exercised by nonbanks include drawing from a large pool of multiple investors to create sizeable amounts of capital available for lending. This practice has led many private lenders into becoming the powerful nonbank commercial lending sources of today with qualifying requirements that resemble those of major banks. Many of these private lenders follow their larger counterparts and require full documentation, significant personal financials, tax returns, and other documents traditional banks were known to require.

Several private lenders can lend at near-bank rates with the ability to minimize risk by increasing those same rates arising from projects that would otherwise never qualify for traditional financing. Non-bank lenders for some may prove to be the right choice.

For Those with Questions About Dodd-Frank

The primary objective of the Dodd-Frank Act is to protect consumers, and therefore is applicable to residential mortgage lending. Business and commercial property transactions typically do not fall under the purview of Dodd-Frank.

Dodd-Frank does not apply to loans secured by vacant land, commercial properties, rental properties or properties used for investment purposes.

Chapter 3

Construction Lending

Conducting financial due diligence in construction lending requires a basic knowledge of construction loans and practices, both of which will be addressed in this chapter. First is a discussion of the process and types of loans available. Second, how construction loans are valued and the need for a quality business plan. Third, you'll learn what red flags to look for when encountering suspicious activity such as vendor fraud.

The Loan Process

The construction loan process begins when a developer submits a loan request to the lender. At one time, developers sought funding from the local community or regional banks. Nowadays, larger banks, even foreign banks, and private debt funds are very active in this field. As in previous years, each lender's interest still depends on the size of the loan, location, and the appetite to do the deal.

Historically, bank regulations restricted several areas of lending. Recently, however, life insurance companies, national banks, and other specialty finance companies have also started making construction loans. Mostly, community and regional banks continue to provide the majority of construction financing.

Lenders of interest are those lenders that have over time, built relationships with developers, which has provided a better understanding of local market conditions and trends. In addition, these same lenders know the backstory and reputation of most local real estate developers and subcontractors.

Starting the Process

The four major types of costs when planning a project are:

1. <u>Hard costs</u> - Direct construction labor and materials costs

2. <u>Land costs</u> - The cost of acquiring land and property with the idea that land purchases may fall under soft costs.

3. <u>Soft costs</u> - The administrative costs to include:

- Permitting
- Architectural design
- Engineering Taxes Insurance (liability, builder's risk, title policy and contingency policy, among others)
- Construction bonding, testing and inspections
- Developer's fee or broker's commission
- Appraisal
- Legal fees
- Interest on construction payments

4. <u>Contingency or reserves</u>:

A reserve or contingency fund must be kept at all times to make interest payments and keep the project solvent. Lenders may require a certain reserve level, typically 5% of hard costs.

Financing

Normally, two possibly three loans are required to finance a real estate development project. Most often these loans will run consecutively, but certain lenders may elect to combine the loans. They are:

<u>Short-term financing (Construction loans)</u>. This stage of financing, funds the construction and lease-up phase of the project and is often replaced by long-term financing.

<u>Mini-perm or Construction financing</u> is used until a project has been completed and can therefore start producing income. A developer will likely use this method of financing before seeking long-term or permanent

financing. We cannot rule out the fact that construction and mini-perm loans are often combined.

Permanent (LT) financing. After a project achieves "stabilization" and leases up to the market level of occupancy, the construction loan is "taken out" by longer-term financing.

Underwriting

During the underwriting process, the lender will usually evaluate:

- The project's proforma
- Details of the construction budget
- Local market conditions
- The owner/developer
- Financial capacity of the guarantors
- Any other risks inherent or discovered in the loan request.

Documents typically required in the underwriting process include: tax returns, financial statements, a schedule of real estate and contingent liabilities for the guarantor(s), the proposed project's proforma, construction loan sources and uses, cost estimates, full project plans, engineering specifications, and other documents that can support the loan request.

Formulas Used when Evaluating a Project

There are several methods used to evaluate the costs or benefits of a project. A few of the most commonly used include:

Net Present Value

The net present value method (NPV) of evaluating a major project allows for the calculation of the project's value based on future cash flows less the initial investment. By adding together future net incomes, assuming a discount factor, the NPV method helps the lender find the present value in "today's dollars" from the projected future net cash flow of a project. This allows the lender to compare the calculated amount with the amount of money needed to implement the project.

Often, lenders will take into consideration the following two hypotheticals in their decision when calculating what they believe is an accurate NPV:

Does the NPV; (1) include a sale in years 7 thru 10 at a cap rate of current + 100 to 150 bps; and (2) Is the discount factor being used, the 10-year Treasury plus 50 to 75 bps?

Internal Rate of Return

Very similar to the NPV, the equity provider will use the internal rate of return (IRR) method to analyze the project's viability by assessing its future income. Usually, the project's IRR must exceed the cost of capital by an agreed amount so that the risk of proceeding is acceptable. Again, calculating the internal rate of return considering only the project cash flows (excluding the financing cash flows) gives us the project's IRR.

Loan to Value and Loan to Cost

*Loan-to-value as it's applied to "**completed**" income-producing properties.*

Commercial property appraisers and underwriters find determining the value for an existing apartment complex relatively simple. What also fits into this category are office buildings or retail centers that are fully occupied and have been in operation for several years. Using the income approach requires a current rent roll, the statement of operating expenses, and the applicable cap rate. Keep in mind, lease rollover and the money necessary to improve property or capital expenditures (CAPEX) are additional factors worthy of consideration.

*Loan-to-value as it's applied to income properties "**under construction**."*

For an income property that has yet to be built, the task becomes more daunting as the appraiser must come up with a realistic number sometimes 18 to 24 months in advance. The appraiser bases his/her decision on the perceived future value of the property, the time required to fully lease up the property; the expenses associated with the process to include marketing, financing and operating costs besides the level of competition in the area.

*Loan-to-cost is a term used primarily with "**construction loans**."*

The Loan-to-cost or LTC represents the amount the lender will advance or lend the borrower regarding the amount of costs associated with construction until the project has been completed. Lenders will traditionally finance up to 65% or 70% of the construction costs. The calculation of the loan to cost value involves using numbers obtained from the "sources and uses" schedule found within the construction budget.

Does the Borrower have "Skin" in the Deal?

With the high number of projects looking for funding, one question will always remain. And that is, "How Much money does the borrower have invested into the project?" Regardless of best-case scenarios, the bottom line is "What Does the borrower bring to the table"?

The belief held by many is that the borrower needs to have "skin in the game" and that's because personal exposure of the borrower usually means the project is more likely to be successful.

Is it collateral, a patent, experience, or is it cash? Is the borrower part of a bigger development group? Are they willing to guarantee the project? Is the collective experience detailed? What is the collateral? And lastly, has the project been clearly presented?

Regardless of best-case scenarios, the bottom line is "What Does the borrower bring to the table"?

Reviewing Major Tenant Financials

As discussed earlier, an understanding of basic credit analysis is important when raising debt financing for commercial real estate projects. While the credit analysis is an important step in the borrower's approval, the lender makes a similar effort when evaluating the financial strength of the proposed major tenants. An example of "what can go wrong" is clear because of the large number of stand-alone retail stores that have recently closed their doors due to higher rents, pulling back or downsizing.

While the credit analysis is an important step in the approval of the borrower, the lender often makes a similar effort when evaluating the financial strength of the proposed major tenants.

Evaluate the Project not the Borrower

Ratios such as debt/equity along with others are used daily to evaluate borrowers who apply for commercial loans on existing properties. While they are valuable, the proposed construction of income properties by real estate development firms requires a different approach. In these cases, relying solely upon ratios will be far less beneficial compared to examining the developer's financial statements. The lender or bank's analysis department will focus on the project's feasibility or the perceived overall success of the project in the making of its decision to lend.

The Feasibility Study

The feasibility study is an analysis and evaluation of the proposed project to determine if it's: (1) technically and economically workable, (2) that the project can be built within the estimated cost, and (3) will the project "based on the analysis" be profitable.

Feasibility studies differ as to their application. They can be included as part of an independent appraisal or as a separate analysis. Many hotel projects use valuation companies that are familiar and respected within the industry. Banks and lenders realize a certain bias exists from feasibility studies provided by the borrower. While studies and appraisals provide insight, they are most helpful in providing the bank with up to date market trends, relative costs, comparisons and area reports. However, many banks even when provided with this information will conduct its own analysis of the project.

Regardless of the total cost to build and market a property, the value of an income-producing property depends largely on the expected Net Operating Income or NOI.

The lender when performing its valuation will consider both the expected costs and the NOI. If in the lenders' determination the total construction costs closely mirror or slightly exceed the expected value of the project's income, they may deem the project too risky and no longer a viable project.

Business Plans

Business plans created using information to include marketing data and other information provided from feasibility studies or other third-parties demand the appropriate attention in order to verify the plan's validity and correctness. Items related to revenue streams from parking, hotel rooms, office rentals, banquet halls, restaurants, and other retail establishments without saying, require a closer look.

As a writer of business plans myself, I highly recommend a comparison of "like" or similar properties within or adjacent to the proposed location. In addition, numbers provided for operational expenses such as electricity, water, gas, and sewer should always be cross-checked by contacting local utility companies.

- Obtain price quotes from companies that offer parking services.
- Survey area hotels offering similar amenities to determine ADR (Average Daily Rate) by season.
- Speak with commercial realtors and local chambers of commerce regarding office space, retail and restaurant (lease costs) per square feet.
- Check with a title company to verify property size, zoning, and ownership. Regarding development property in foreign countries, it may be necessary to check with local government officials regarding ownership, property grants, and use.
- Who is the architect? How are they being paid? Is it a percentage of building costs? And what have they determined as the cost to build?
- Who is the general contractor? What is their experience, bonding, etc.?
- Check with local building departments regarding permits, special needs, entitlements, and compliance.

Preparing the Business Plan: Experience counts!

My experience in the writing of more than $800 million in commercial real estate-related business plans has led me to believe:

Having a first-class presentation is a definite step in the right direction in securing a multimillion-dollar loan. The knowledgeable borrower may even go a step further and have the consultant stay on-site for at least a week to formulate his or her own understanding of the developer's business.

The experienced consultant should make recommendations and encourage both dialog and feedback. Seldom, has the "perfect" business operation existed. Most times, even the astute borrower will miss secondary sources of income and in some cases submit poorly constructed financials, not to mention a business plan that does not include a well thought out "Exit

Strategy." If you're still unsure, then find out why so many brokers and lenders continue to ask for more and more items?

Books and software packages do not replace engaging the services of an experienced business plan writer. To be clear, as a business plan writer myself, I do not view nor even consider cousins or nephews (or other relatives in fact) who've completed an ESL course as a credible alternative. A true business plan writer knows what lenders are looking for and possesses the knowledge to create a presentation in the manner and format that receives proper attention.

The right consultant is one who's an excellent writer of English or in the language in which funding is sought. Besides being a good writer, the consultant must have the financial background to create the most effective business plan. The first impression is obviously a lasting impression.

Books and software packages do not replace engaging the services of an experienced professional writer of business plans.

Important Steps to Follow When Writing a Business Plan

Items that must be referenced within the "first two pages" of the business plan are:

- Who is the borrower, what is it they do, how long have they been doing it, and what are their accomplishments?
- What is the project and its intended uses?
- Where is the project to be located?
- How much money is needed to complete the project and what is the borrower's contribution?
- How and where will the borrowed money be spent?
- What are the benefits to the community to include jobs, income, and taxes?
- How do the borrowers intend to repay the loan? Will there be an offering of equity, Will they seek a take-out loan, or a mix of both?

*Sometimes the Best Decision is not to Rebuild but to Build Something
Different*

While on assignment in Mexico, someone asked me to inspect and render
an opinion on a resort and hotel on the east cape north of Cabo San
Jose. While the proposed buyer's first intention was to build residential
homes and a golf course inland of the coastal highway, the plan also
included the purchase of the seaside resort across the road which would
provide residents with access to the beach.

On my initial inspection, I found the resort older, showing its age, but yet
possessed several very nice amenities such as; a beautiful pool, bar area,
restaurant, beach, conference center, and a nice hotel. What blocked the
amazing view between the pool and the new hotel was an older dilapidated
two-story building that once accommodated the resort's employees or
possibly even guests. Besides, the same building was blocking the view of
the beach from the conference center.

The buyer was interested in maintaining the historic feel of the property
but didn't quite know what to do with this building. The plan at the time
was to renovate the building at an enormous cost. I proposed two
options:

A.) First, if the buyer stayed with the original plan and were to invest good
money into this older building, the result would be a nice-looking older
building with guest rooms that were too small by today's standards.

B.) The suggestion I left him with was to tear down the existing structure,
leaving just the concrete foundation. From there, the buyer could construct
an outdoor dining and reception area. The changes would allow hotel
guests to view the pool and bar while looking through the newly built open
cabana-styled reception area. Visitors to the conference center would have
a new facility to hold outdoor events, business retreats, and other social
activities. The addition of a small white beach gazebo in front of the new
reception area would bring in additional sources of revenues from wedding
parties and receptions.

Overall, the cost to build something new was far less compared to the
renovation costs of an older two-story building that had outlived its
usefulness. The point the buyer quickly understood was that the resort did

not need more rooms (and the costs to maintain such) but a new low-cost structure which would generate several additional sources of revenue for the resort.

The Need for Construction Monitoring

For all intents and purposes, construction loans while creating new jobs also finance the creation of collateral. Repayment or takeout of the construction loan is dependent on the project's completion. Here are a few factors that would pose serious threats to the project's success.

• Fraudulent diversion of draws can and will pose a problem. To curb the possibility of fraud, monthly draws can be set up and made through escrow, funding subcontractors individually.

• Liens filed by contractors, subcontractors, or material suppliers for nonpayment can be an issue. Again, many of these problems can be alleviated through proper monitoring.

• Delays caused by labor disputes or the failure of major suppliers to deliver materials on schedule are difficult to predict or plan for in the predevelopment process.

• Failure of the contractor or subcontractor to complete construction or complete the project to desired specifications if not routinely monitored can become a reality and costly problem. Much of this may be due to inadequate experience, negligence, or financial failure. These problems, for the most part, can be preempted by way of proper due diligence (analysis discipline) of the contracting parties during the bidding and award process. Also, proper bonding and required guarantees can limit both liability and risk.

• Cost overruns are primarily due to unforeseen conditions, such as: poorly constructed or inaccurate budgets, increases in materials or transportation costs, labor shortages, increased interest expense, inadequate soil or other subsurface conditions, or delays caused by inclement weather. Each of the aforementioned are non-dependent and by themselves can create serious issues for all parties concerned. These problems often lead to further rescheduling if not increased spending by the developer and builder and heightened concern by the lender.

Proper and timely monitoring through reconciliation and verification of invoices and their payment is also important. As a manner of doing so and consistently following-up, the lender should insist on a "monthly cost to complete analysis." Besides the analysis, and as one of the loan covenants, the lender should reserve the legal right to halt or suspend funding requiring an equity "top-up" or cash infusion from developer equal in amount to the calculated cost overrun.

Problems, for the most part, can be prevented by way of proper due diligence (analysis discipline) of the contracting parties during the bidding and award process.

Issues to be Mindful of Regarding General Contractors

Asset Misappropriation

According to the Association of Certified Fraud Examiners' 2016 Report to the Nations on Occupational Fraud and Abuse, construction companies endured a median loss of $259,000 per reported incident. In 2018, the number decreased by $32,000 to $227,000. While the reported losses are less, any loss is problematic!

Asset Misappropriation occurs when an employee uses the company's assets, such as cash, inventory, tools, equipment or materials for reasons other than its intended purpose. One requisite of construction related financial due diligence is the reconciliation of accounts by the matching of purchase orders, receipts, payments and invoices for materials ordered and received.

Just as important, we should never discount job site security. Depending on the location, adequate fencing and cameras may sometimes not be enough. Determine if on-site security is required on around the clock basis if not nightly as needed. Find out what safeguards and releases are in place to protect tools and equipment from leaving the premises without authorization?

Use of Substandard Materials

Many countries have established national building codes and material specification guidelines. History has shown that both here in the United States and abroad, numerous instances have been reported where substandard materials were improperly substituted as a cost-savings measure. These decisions often led to the structural failure of the building's integrity, and yet many of the structural problems were discovered only after incidents of earthquakes or fire.

Some of the areas where substandard materials have been found, include; faulty wiring, watered-down cement, improper use of reinforcement steel and ill-fitted plumbing.

Counterfeit Parts

The fraudulent use of counterfeit parts most often applies to construction projects and manufacturing. Contractors are continually being duped into buying excellent imitations (of lesser quality) of required building materials. These items can range in size from something as small as an electrical breaker to as big as a fire sprinkler control valve or a truckload of seamless pipe. The odd packaging can often identify these parts via modified labeling or markings.

Insist on matching invoices for materials from suppliers. Hopefully, the vendors encountered are on the "approved" list. If possible, learn what vendors and suppliers need to know.

Substandard Workmanship

Besides the use of substandard materials, falsified inspection reports by a subcontractor back in 2008 led to the stoppage of construction of the planned 49 story luxury Harmon Hotel in Las Vegas. According to the

ACFE, estimated costs of the failed project were at $279 million, plus another $2 million in the dismantling.

In all cases, the contractor must abide by the terms of the contract, especially if a signed detailed construction contract is in place which specifies the nature, brand, type, or quality of materials that a contractor must use. If a project requires changes, all parties to the agreement should sign off on the change of material selected and a written update to the contract should be made. Contractors acting alone should never be allowed to substitute in different materials. In fact, all changes should be accompanied by the project owner's signature and recorded.

If the choice of materials places even one person at risk of harm or causes actual injury, then grounds may exist in making a claim for damages due to the use of inadequate or unsafe building materials. For example, a contractor who substituted in low-quality drywall susceptible to mold problems which caused respiratory issues, could possibly be held liable.

Undocumented Workers

A 2017 Pew Research Center study reported that of the roughly 10 million U.S. construction workers, 15% are undocumented immigrants and another 12% are not U.S. citizens but are immigrants here legally. About 21% of adult undocumented workers in California work in construction, according to the University of Southern California Center for the Study of Immigrant Rights.

Herein lies the problem; it's illegal to hire undocumented workers, yet many contractors looking to reduce labor costs continue to do so. It's also safe to assume a great number of undocumented workers have several years of experience. However, many of these same undocumented workers lack proper training; and it's the absence of proper training that has led to problems such as the improper installation of certain materials, "do-overs," or sometimes leaving the worker susceptible to injury while performing their assigned task.

Red Flags Associated with Project Development (Warnings or dangers of a problem)

- Finding charges for non-allowable costs
- Failure to deliver on the project's contracted scope
- Lost incentives and credits
- Overcharging for labor and materials
- Overpriced change orders
- Risk Factors (Coming from sources both internal and external to the organization)
- Bonuses for estimators, project managers, purchasing agents and supervisors, dependent on specific criteria.
- Tax-motivated income or loss goals
- Ownership dispute, a potential sale, divorce
- Owner expectation and demand for income
- Manipulation of contract schedule
- Disregard for authority or regulations
- Continued employment of under-qualified accounting personnel
- Frequent change in external auditors
- Frequent or recent change in banking or bonding
- Inability of management to accurately project gross profit in the past.
- Presence of OSHA fines and no safety program
- Pressure to meet loan covenants or bonding equity requirements
- Cash flow difficulties
- Interest rates on current debts are higher than the industry average.
- Significant claims or unapproved change orders
- Contractors that collect or use significant amounts of cash
- Lack of owner or management oversight
- Inadequate record keeping over company procedures
- Lack of procedures for allowing and approving transactions

Reducing many of these risks is accomplished by:

- Conducting weekly budget reviews
- Periodic review by a qualified construction auditor/consultant

Chapter 4

Various Methods Used to Commit Commercial Real Estate Fraud

What is Commercial Real Estate Fraud?

Commercial real estate fraud takes on many forms. Unlike most fraudulent schemes found in business involving one or two perpetrators at best, fraud in commercial real estate usually involves multiples of people, to include appraisers, accountants and brokers.

The most common type of real estate fraud is the misappropriation of funds. This happens when borrowers knowingly divert funds obtained from a loan or payment received towards the completion of a project. For instance, you do the right thing by paying rent for the property that houses your business. Then, instead of paying the lender, the property owner uses the same funds meant to pay the mortgage to pay for capital improvements on another property. This could qualify as a misappropriation of funds, especially if the mortgage on the initial property goes unpaid or continues to be delinquent.

Commercial real estate fraud, besides the misappropriation of funds, frequently involves misrepresentations. This fraud is accomplished through the submission of falsified documents, false statements or providing fraudulent financial statements. In other words, a potential borrower may provide fabricated appraisals accompanied by inflated financial statements. This is usually done to bolster his or her loan application in order to receive a favorable answer. In actuality, the borrower may not qualify for the loan nor even have the ability to fulfill subsequent obligations should they receive the loan.

SARs and the Financial Crimes Enforcement Network (FinCEN)

The Financial Crimes Enforcement Network (FinCEN) released an analysis in 2011 of suspicious activity reports (SARs) that call attention to possible fraud in commercial real estate. By definition, a Suspicious Activity Report (or SAR) is a document that financial institutions must file with the Financial Crimes Enforcement Network (FinCEN) following a suspected incident of money laundering or fraud. These reports are required under the United States Bank Secrecy Act (BSA) of 1970.

The top four reported categories by the FinCen in order are: False Documents, Misappropriation of Funds, Collusion-Bank Insider, and False Statements. The FinCEN reported that approximately half of the SARs pertaining to commercial real estate named subjects residing in five states: Georgia, Illinois, Florida, New York, and California.

The commercial Real Estate (CRE) market includes brokerage and lending services for the industrial, retail, office, hotel, and multi-family housing sectors. Special Activity Reports related to the CRE market involve a variety of transactions and activities related to the purchase and development of raw land as well as the acquisition, development, construction, and improvement of commercial buildings.

Examples of fraud or illicit activity reported in SAR's included borrowers who reportedly sold CRE collateral without disclosure to the lender or pledged the same assets for multiple purposes, often hiding the conveyed collateral from associates.

Upon review, (SAR's) reports found that much of the commercial real estate financing fraud had originated from institutions of varying sizes and locations; an indicator that fraud associated with financing of commercial real estate affected a broad range of lending institutions. Further analysis found that in many of the reported cases, fraudulent financial documents supporting the various loan applications were discovered only after other suspicious activities occurred.

The SAR must be filed no later than 30 calendar days after the date of initial detection of facts that may constitute a basis for the filing. Financial institutions have to keep a copy of the SAR and the original or business record of any supporting documentation for five years. Federal law requires that a financial institution and its directors, officers, employees and agents who report suspected or known criminal violations or suspicious activity may <u>not notify</u> any of the named persons involved in the report.

Predominant Methods Used to Commit Real Estate Fraud

Commercial real estate transactions and their complexity, particularly those involving investors, offer ample opportunity for the intelligent but corrupt individual(s) to commit fraud. For instance, corrupt real estate investors understand the "ins and outs" of transactions, and may have the "know-how" to defraud banks. Fraudulent appraisals, corrupt mortgage brokers and straw buyers all play a role in perpetrating real estate fraud.

Several examples exist of suspected CRE fraud involving commercial property, including land, condominiums, office buildings, stores, hotels, and even single-family homes. The subjects of these fraudulent activities often include individuals that are either lenders, bank insiders, commercial real estate industry insiders, construction companies, or commercial loan borrowers.

Methods included in this discussion are:

Misrepresentations

Occur when false statements are made and/or falsified documents including: rent rolls, tax documentation, appraisals, draw requests, lien waivers, and financial statements are submitted. In a majority of cases, these fraudulent statements or falsified documents are given to lenders in order to bolster loan applications. Unscrupulous or crooked borrowers have been known to make repeated fraudulent requests for disbursement, including the submission of fake invoices and other receipts in order to receive loan proceeds. Lenders have reported that many of the same borrowers have previously used similar scams to defraud other banks.

Misappropriation of funds

Occur when borrowers purposely misappropriate or divert borrowed funds to other projects. The activity is often observed when a borrower files for bankruptcy or when lenders perform site inspections.

Non-Disclosure

Non-Disclosure occurs when corrupt borrowers purposely avoid giving key information to lenders affecting lending decisions. A common example is the non-disclosure of a debt such as a preexisting mortgage which has intentionally been omitted from current or year-end financial statements. Additional problems arise when unethical borrowers do not inform lenders when properties are either sold or transferred. Oftentimes, these same borrowers are engaged in side agreements with questionable property buyers.

Document forgery

To qualify for a loan, an investor or their co-conspirators may forge key documents to present a "brighter" but untrue financial picture. These activities include altering bank statements and other financial documents, such as balance sheets and profit & loss statements. An investor might also misrepresent his or her financial position by failing to disclose all relevant assets and liabilities.

Phony or inflated appraisal

Because inflating a real estate asset's value increases the chances the loan application will receive approval, shady real estate investors might seek incompetent or unethical appraisers. Alternatively, the same investor might offer the appraiser a kickback to inflate the appraised value. Instead of paying a bribe, the crooked real estate investor could provide the appraiser with altered or overly optimistic information, such as unrealistic vacancy rates, rental rates, and expenses.

Bank insider collusion

Is a very real concept! Bank insiders have reportedly played essential roles in facilitating the loan approval process and the disbursement of funds. In fact, bank insider collusion has been alleged in cases where the suspected bank insider (sometimes an officer or director) has breached multiple bank policies and procedures. These same bank insiders are often involved in acts of bribery and are known to be colluding with borrowers and/ or other real estate insiders. In several instances, the client base of certain "bank insiders" has moved with them as they have changed employment.

Flipping

Property flipping as we know it from watching television is legal; but when it's done for ill-gotten gain it becomes a crime. Flipping becomes a fraudulent act when recently acquired property is resold for a considerable profit using an artificially inflated value. The fraud begins when an investor purchases a piece of property and then quickly resells it at an artificially inflated price to a co-conspirator or straw buyer who has no intention of paying the mortgage. The original buyer gets involved and pays off the first loan, while he or she splits the proceeds of the second loan with the straw buyer who makes no attempt to repay the new mortgage. Eventually, the bank forecloses on the loan, which now far exceeds the actual value of the property.

Short-sale scheme

Short-sale schemes differ from flipping in that the borrower sells the property for a price that is less than the total debt owed. The lender agrees to release its lien on the property and to accept the proceeds of the sale in full or partial satisfaction of the outstanding indebtedness. The scheme is accomplished when the original investor uses a straw buyer to purchase the property. The straw buyer then defaults. Low and behold, just before the bank forecloses, the first investor steps in to purchase the property from the straw buyer during the short sale (an amount less than the mortgage balance, with the bank forgiving the shortfall). Due to the straw buyer's default, the original investor repurchases the property well below market value.

Collateral transfer

Collateral transfer is best described as transfers or sale of real property (pledged collateral) by borrowers without disclosure to the lender. In many cases, borrowers either did not report the sale or forward the proceeds of the collateral sale to the lender. In fact, these same borrowers may have conveyed the (pledged) collateral to associates and sometimes, quit-claim deeded the collateral to another entity. In several instances, transfers of ownership have been made to family members or trust accounts. Banks have reported that borrowers have intentionally diverted funds for collateral improvements to other projects or falsely inflated collateral values, which have negatively affected the banks' financial position.

Advance Fee Schemes

Advance fee fraud is best described as a scheme that targets borrowers. In doing this, unethical lenders, brokers and sometimes others will attempt to collect fees, sometimes large amounts upfront from the borrower for their help in securing a loan. In reality, the scheme is played out on those who typically would not qualify for conventional CRE financing. The advance fee scheme in particular, often involves the submission of fraudulent business proposals and financial instruments.

The Pitfalls of Money Laundering

The U.S. government reportedly spends $16.8 billion annually through the United States Agency for International Development (USAID) to fund programs in developing countries. However, many of the recipients have ties to corrupt politicians and criminal organizations who later export billions of these dollars to be invested in real estate abroad in a growing, global money-laundering racket. Money laundering in real estate (MLRE) is and has been a growing problem in both developed and developing countries.

Accuity, a global risk and compliance company reported that real estate-related money laundering schemes are estimated to reach $1.6 trillion in 2019.   One method includes opening bank accounts in Europe with ill-gotten money and by using a direct funds wire, money is then sent from the European bank directly into a U.S. based escrow account in order to close cash purchases on one or more properties. Finally, a subsequent loan is taken on the properties to obtain cash on a tax-free basis.

Understand that money laundering and tax evasion by means of real estate transactions often go hand in hand.

Real estate is often the preferred destination for the financial criminal as the market for real estate is stable and usually appreciates. Real estate is also functional; a money launderer could use the property and potentially earn income from the investment.

For years, unethical real estate investors have used a similar approach for purchases of commercial properties and this is precisely why commercial property transactions are uniquely vulnerable to money laundering. Purchases of commercial property is ideal because the size of these transactions can involve moving a significant amount of money at one time.

In the U.S., real estate agents and lawyers aren't required to have anti-money-laundering (AML) initiatives — they don't have to conduct due diligence on transactions or report suspicious activity. At the same time, many of the commercial real estate purchases are made through LLCs formed specifically to purchase and own property. Real estate buyers usually LLC's can be composed of individuals, families, trusts or shell companies whose ownership is hard to determine. Actual owners of some LLC's may not be fully disclosed in the operating agreements and the domestic agents forming the LLC's may be cut-outs for the real owners.

As of February 2018, there had been no regulatory obligations imposed on title or escrow providers (or on attorneys handling transactions in non-escrow states) to validate the origin of funds coming through a direct wire from an offshore bank account. As of this writing, regulatory measures have not been imposed on brokerage firms, which would force them to investigate offshore parties wishing to open a U.S. bank account. Both politicians and regulators recognize the lackadaisical response in our money laundering defense network and despite the level of regulation in place on banks and deposit transactions, there has been little to no effort in closing the loophole in commercial real estate transactions.

All-cash deals for real estate purchases are not uncommon and can be done without involving many parties beyond an agent and a lawyer.

Ease of Cash Conversion

The U.S. Treasury in 2016 finally enacted regulations forcing title companies to disclose all cash transactions between $1,500,000 and $3,000,000 that were completed in the States of New York, Florida, California, and Texas. The keyword here is disclosed or report, not investigate! No such regulations have been imposed on other states, and the $3,000,000 number mandated for disclosure often falls short of the sizable and more complex commercial property deals. Let it be known that as of November 2018, real estate agents were still exempt from filing.

To Ask or Not Ask?

No broker I can think of wants to be involved in either an ethics or criminal investigation and the broader regulations regarding full disclosure if imposed on the offshore buyer would likely create a new set of problems of its own. The broker to be compliant fully understands the many personal questions that could be asked of the offshore buyer and if this were to happen, we could expect to see the following:

a.) the number of international investors would be reduced, and

b.) the processing of loans would require a longer period of time.

In the end, all-cash deals would be fewer, resulting in a smaller number of closed deals. Thus, fewer commissions.

Red Flags

Brokers and others in the real estate industry who work with international buyers need to know what situations to be aware of. The following points should raise a red flag:

Size of transaction — A real estate purchase that is substantially higher or lower than the average market value of the property could indicate the transaction has purposes other than just acquiring a property.

Location of property — A real estate purchase in a particular geographic area known for a history of questionable activity is a red flag. These areas range from popular, high-appreciation markets like New York and London to lesser areas covered by a FinCEN GTO. For example, Bexar County, Texas is considered to be a popular location for Mexican cartels to buy property.

Location of buyer — If the buyer is a shell company based in a country with a history of money-laundering activities, such as the British Virgin Islands or Mauritius, they should merit greater scrutiny.

Disparity between buyer, bank and property location — A sign of possible fraud is when a company in one location sends a wire transfer from an institution in a high-risk location to buy a property in a third location. For example, if a customer is an international company in Spain that sends a wire transfer from an account in the British Virgin Islands for a condo purchase in Manhattan, that should be a red flag.

An offshore buyer — who intends to make an all-cash purchase. Money launderers don't want to deal with lenders who will ask all kinds of questions, so the transactions are almost always all-cash.

The purchase is in an amount over $5 million. The Treasury regulations in the few states mentioned above only scrutinize transactions topping out at $3 million, so larger purchases are not disclosed to the U.S. Treasury Department.

The purchase funds will be wired directly from an offshore source to a U.S. escrow account and not through a U.S. bank account maintained by the buyers. Again, money is being wired to an escrow account and not to a bank.

The buyers don't have a U.S. bank account. This is the biggest red flag of all. If a bank has conducted their own (Know Your Client) KYC process and opened an account for the buyer, this would indicate the buyer has passed the bank KYC investigation and the presumption is, the buyer is a legitimate player. However, if the buyer does not have a U.S. bank account, that would be a red flag and worthy of investigation.

Remember, suspicion is raised when buyers do not have a U.S. bank account.

Form 8300

The Form 8300 must be filed by a business that receives more than $10,000 in cash in the course of a single transaction or two or more related transactions. It is not a Suspicious Activity Report (SAR) and is not used to report suspicious activity. Form 8300 is an information report that is required to be filed by any trade or business (such as a car or boat dealer) that receives in excess of $10,000 in cash in a single transaction. Therefore, if for any reason a real estate agent or broker receives more than $10,000 in cash from a buyer or seller in the course of a real estate transaction, the form must be filled out and filed.

Penalties for Money Laundering

Money laundering fines can be steep. While misdemeanor convictions typically allow for fines of a few thousand dollars, a federal conviction for money laundering can result in fines of up to $500,000 or double the amount of money that was laundered, whichever is greater. And if the court wishes, they can levy a combination of jail time and a fine.

In California, the lowest form of money laundering is misdemeanor money laundering and carries with it the following penalties:

- Up to one year in either county jail or state prison.

- No more than $1,000.
- Combination of jail time and a fine.

California defendants facing felony money laundering charges, the consequences are more intense:

- A minimum sentence of 16 months and up to four years in jail.
- A fine of $250,000 or twice the amount of money laundered. For the purposes of calculating the fine, the court imposes the higher of the two amounts.
- Combination of jail time and a fine.

Issues of Wire Fraud in Commercial Real Estate

Each year, thousands of Americans fall victim to real estate wire fraud. In all areas of real estate, including commercial, wire fraud has been on the rise. As noted in a 2018 Housingwire.com blog, in 2016, there was a 480 percent increase in wire fraud scams reported by title companies to the Internet Crime Complaint Center (IC3). The article also mentioned that in the same year, wire fraud scammers targeted nearly $5.3 billion in the (real estate) mortgage industry. Unfortunately, this fraud shows no signs of slowing down for 2019.

In 2015, Tom Cronkright, President at Sun Title, found himself a victim of fraud, losing more than $180,000 on a commercial real estate investment. Though he's since recovered his money (after testifying before the Department of Justice and taking down part of an African crime syndicate, no less), the fraud left a lasting mark. Cronkright now speaks about real estate wire fraud across the country, helping to educate consumers and industry players on its dangers, how to prevent it, and what to do if you should fall victim.

According to the FBI, the real estate industry both residential and commercial experienced a 1,100% increase in the number of victims that reported attacks and a 2,200% rise in reported monetary losses between 2015 and 2017.

Commercial real estate as an industry has become a major target for those committing cyber-crime. There's no question that technology has streamlined the commercial real estate process. Information or documents that used to take days to distribute via courier can now be transmitted to your computer or even your mobile device in a matter of seconds.

To support this argument, Ryan Terry of Proofpoint, a California-based cybersecurity specialist said that, "Cybercriminals continue to target the real estate industry because its high-value transactions occur frequently and take place digitally." Terry went on to say that "According to (their) research, in the last quarter (2018), 14% of attackers went after the real estate CFO, while nearly 9% went after procurement personnel and 9%, the human resources department."

Bisnow.com reported in 2019 that email fraud attacks on real estate companies by those attempting to steal information or install a malware on their computers was on the rise. During the third quarter of 2018, real estate companies sustained an average 54 attacks per company.

The sheer number of real estate transactions involving several parties affords fraudsters multiple opportunities to commit fraud. Such methods include the use of email account types such as: web mail, registered vanity domains, broker domains, etc.

The use of various internet methods can make it difficult in determining what's legitimate and what's fraudulent.

As hackers obtain sensitive information regarding real estate transactions, real estate professionals need to take measures to protect their clients and themselves from wire fraud.

How Wire Fraud is Perpetrated

Wire fraud involves hackers breaking into email accounts of real estate agents to obtain details regarding upcoming transactions. The email account could belong to a real estate agent, attorney, even an underwriter. In fact, anyone involved in the transaction could be a target. Once hackers get the information, they pose as an agent or title company representative and contact the buyer.

The hacker states in the email to the buyer, that a change in the closing instructions has occurred and the buyer needs to follow the new wire instructions which is often a request for additional money. If the buyer follows the new instructions, they could possibly be saying farewell to a sizeable sum of money.

Red Flags

An indicator of wire fraud can be as simple as an email that refers to a Society for Worldwide Interbank Financial Telecommunication or SWIFT account requesting a wire transfer of funds from your account to be sent to an overseas account.

Many of these fraudulent emails include detailed information pertaining to a specific real estate transaction. These fraudsters having access to the agent's email account often leave unsuspicious buyers confused, assuming the email is from a legitimate source. Email addresses often appear legitimate because the hacker has created a fake email account using the name of the real estate company or because they've hacked the agent's actual email account.

Pay attention to the red flags commonly associated with compromised emails, such as:

- Misspellings
- Poor grammar. Many Nigerian scams will use a small letter "i" in place of a capital I.
- A sense of urgency requesting emails to be sent outside of normal business hours.
- Modifications in payment type, such as changing from a certified check to a wire transfer, or account numbers that were revised at the last minute.

How to Avoid Wire Fraud

Wire fraud is one of several types of online fraud targeting real estate professionals and their clients. To prevent cyber-crime from occurring, every party involved in the real estate transaction needs to implement and follow a standard set of security measures:

- Never send wire transfer instructions or any sensitive information via email. This includes financial information.
- Inform clients about your email and communication practices and explain that you will never ask nor expect them to send sensitive information via email.
- If wiring funds, start by contacting the recipient using a verified phone number to confirm that the wiring information is accurate.
- Ask your bank to confirm not just the account number but also the name on the account before wiring funds.
- If email is the only method available for sending information about a transaction, make sure someone encrypts it.
- Delete old emails regularly, as they may reveal information that hackers can use.
- On a regular basis, change usernames and passwords, and make sure they're difficult to guess. A strong password is accomplished by using numbers, capital letters and special characters.
- Every user nowadays employs (or should) some form of anti-virus technology. Make sure it is up to date and that firewalls are installed and working.

Never open suspicious emails. If the email has already been opened, never click on any of the links in the email, nor open any attachments or even reply to the email.

How the Courts Have Ruled

A Federal Court in 2018 upheld a jury's finding that the real estate agent and broker were 85% responsible for a wire fraud that cost their client $196,622.67 (Bain v. Platinum Realty, LLC, Dist. Court, D. Kansas 2018).

They found both the real estate agent and broker liable for 85% of the wire fraud amount.

According to the backstory, Jerry Bain was working with a real estate agent to purchase a piece of property. To fund the purchase, Bain received wire instructions (no less by the hacker) to wire $196,622.67 to a "title company." However, the money wasn't being wired to the title company but to the fraudster's bank account. Unbeknownst to the parties involved, a criminal was intercepting e-mails exchanged between the title company, agent, and Bain.

Once the funds were sent, they could not be recovered and Bain sued the agent, broker and others.

The court ruled that both the real estate agent and broker were liable. The court emphasized several points:

- The real estate agent served as the middleman between the settlement agent and her client. Serving in this role made her responsible for the delivery of accurate instructions to her client.
- Real Estate agents should not be involved with wire transfer instructions. Buyers and Sellers should communicate directly with the title company.
- The agent did not alert the other parties to the transaction when she learned her e-mail account had been compromised.
- If your email account is compromised, you have an obligation to notify the parties involved. Make sure you notify clients, title companies and lenders promptly.
- If your email account is compromised, you have an obligation to notify the parties involved.

If You Suspect Wire Fraud

If you receive an unexpected or unusual email, forward it to the source it allegedly came from. This will alert everyone involved that there is a possibility of fraudulent activity surrounding their company or the transaction.

If your funds are transferred to a fraudulent account during a commercial real estate transaction, it's imperative that you act quickly to minimize the potential loss. First, contact your bank or financial institution to see if they can start a recall of the funds. Then, reach out to the local office of the FBI. If the transaction just happened, they may help return or freeze the funds. Regardless of the amount that's lost, file a complaint at ic3.gov.

If a buyer falls victim to the scam and wires money to the fraudulent account, they're unlikely to see the money again. Many victims, especially those in the industry, are hesitant to report instances of fraud, fearing possible hits to their reputation. Estimates are that only 15% of all fraud is actually reported. In fact, wire fraud cases have been estimated to exceed well over $10 billion dollars.

Remember, everyone is vulnerable to wire fraud, including attorneys, lenders, agents, title companies, sellers and buyers included.

Don't Fall Prey to Advance Fee Schemes

Advance fee schemes are all too common in commercial real estate ventures. By definition, this scam involves offering financing without the real ability or intention to provide it. For example, the scammer offers to assist a borrower in locating financing. After the borrower has signed a contract and paid a "finder's fee," he learns weeks later that he was never eligible for the financing. By this time, the scammer is long gone or is no longer available to take your calls.

The variety of advance fee fraud schemes is limited only by the imagination of the fraudsters who offer them. Frequently, fraudsters in the commercial real estate arena will offer common financial instruments such as bank guarantees, old government or corporate bonds, medium or long-term notes, standby letters of credit, blocked funds programs, "fresh cut" or "seasoned" paper, and proofs of funds.

These advance fee schemes are designed to mislead investors with official-sounding websites and e-mail addresses. These addresses may contain ".gov" and end in ".us" or ".org." U.S. government agency websites or email addresses end in ".gov," ".mil," or "fed.us." Be wary of a website or correspondence claiming to be from a U.S. government agency if the website or e-mail address does not end in ".gov," ".mil," or "fed.us."

Even if the sender's email address appears to end in ".gov," ".mil," or "fed.us," an impersonator may have emailed the message. Upon receiving such an email, click only on the "details" portion of the sender's address. Doing so may provide the sender's true email address. Often, these addresses do not match.

The Financial Crimes Enforcement Network (FinCEN) describes Advance Fee Schemes as those involving fraudulent business proposals and financial instruments targeting borrowers, lenders, and companies unable to get traditional CRE financing. These activities sometimes directly involve fraudulent financing being offered but not necessarily through a bank.

An example of such is a group of business associates who proposed a scheme in which a bank would purchase U.S. Treasury Bonds and in return receive a letter of credit to finance a large commercial property. The bank recognized the proposal as a potential scam and ceased communications with the group. Another developer reported a request from a broker for a high-dollar loan using properties located outside the United States as collateral to fund various factories. The bank could not confirm that the subject owned the properties and believed the request was fraudulent because of inconsistencies in the information provided.

Another example is a customer who reported that in his attempts to change a commercial mortgage, an unnamed servicing company was perpetrating an advance fee scheme. The bank advised the customer it was a scam when the customer stated that the company would only accept payment sent through a money transmitter.

Guidelines on How to Avoid Advanced Fee Schemes

The SEC's Office of Investor Education and Advocacy offered the following guidelines on how to avoid Advanced Fee Schemes:

"If something seems too good to be true, then it probably is."

Exercise smart business practices.

- Be sure you know who you're trading with. If you aren't familiar with the person or company you plan to do business with, learn more about them. Ask a lot of questions. Visit their location, do your homework, look them up on the internet or with the Better Business Bureau and/or consult with family, friends or an attorney.

- Money spent upfront to pay an attorney to review complex business agreements can save you money in the long run. If you don't understand the terms, have the agreements examined by a knowledgeable and recommended attorney.

- Businesses that operate out of post office boxes, mail drops, and/or don't have a street address should be dealt with suspicion. Also, be leery of those who don't have a direct phone line, can't be reached and must always return your call at a later date and time.

- Be cautious of business deals requiring you to first sign a nondisclosure or non-circumvention agreement before moving forward. These agreements can sometimes prevent you from verifying the legitimacy of those of whom you are doing business with. Scammers tend to use these agreements as a threat of civil litigation against victims should they report the scammer's business activities to law enforcement agencies.

Multi-Family Mortgage Fraud

Many recent examples include cases where building owners have sought loans to either purchase or refinance and in their efforts to do so, have submitted false documentation or had vacant units disguised to appear as occupied.

The increased activity seen in multi-family fraud has been attributed to an overwhelming rise in fraudulent practices.

Common methods used to commit fraud of this type include:

- Falsifying the number of residents (by knowingly providing the lender with a reduced number of vacancies).
- Altered leases or providing leases where there were no tenants.
- Submitting fraudulent income statements and tax returns in order to secure larger loans or gain favorable tax treatment.

Fraudulent tax returns

Selim Zherka, a New York businessman, pled guilty in 2015 to conspiring to make false statements to a bank in order to receive millions of dollars in loans and to file materially false tax returns with the IRS. As part of his plea agreement, Zherka agreed to forfeit $5.23 million.

U.S. Attorney Preet Bharara said Selim Zherka had waged a year-long campaign of lies to a bank and the IRS in order to obtain millions of dollars in loans and fraudulently reduce his tax liabilities.

From 2005 through 2015, Zherka had conspired with others to obtain $63.5 million in loans from Sovereign Bank (now Santander) for the purchase and refinancing of several apartment house complexes in Tennessee. Zherka did this by lying about the purchase price of the real estate he was acquiring and the amounts of the down payments towards the purchases.

In addition, Zherka pled guilty to charges of tax fraud stemming from what authorities believed to be a five-year-long tax fraud scheme. It was alleged that Zherka and his partners repeatedly submitted fraudulent tax returns to the IRS which overstated depreciation expenses and understated his capital gains, thus reducing their tax liabilities.

Knock, Knock...anybody home?

Indicted last year were owners of seven residential multifamily properties in New York and in Pennsylvania who obtained over $167.5 million worth of loans. The fraud they're alleged to have committed was accomplished by tricking the lender into believing the number of vacant units was much fewer than what it actually was. Methods included: turning on radios and placing shoes on doormats outside of vacant apartments. In one case, a woman even told inspectors her boyfriend could not be disturbed as he was inside the apartment and asleep.

According to the DOJ, the individuals involved stood accused of:

- Conspiring to provide lending institutions with false rent rolls suggesting the properties had more occupied units, at higher rental rates, and generated more income then what was actually received.
- Conspiring to provide false information about other income received at the complexes.
- Conspiring to provide lenders with fraudulently altered leases.
- Conspiring to prevent inspectors from touring the properties.

Vitally important to audit vacancies

While it's understandable that commercial lenders are unable to obtain an estoppel certificate from every apartment tenant, lenders should require the appraiser to do an audit of at least 5% to 10% of the apartment units listed on the Rent Roll.

Ponzi Scheme-Like Tactics

In May of 2018, the Wall Street Journal reported that the SEC filed civil charges against Robert Morgan for operating a "Ponzi scheme-like" effort using cash from small investors and misleading banks to get bigger loans by using fake documents. Doing so afforded Morgan and his partners to obtain a $45.8 million loan, which was wrapped into mortgage securities and sold to investors.

In the complaint, Morgan is alleged to have raised more than $110 million from 2013 through September 2018, including $80 million for four specific note funds. According to the SEC, the sale of the securities from within the funds was one of four ways Morgan financed his business. It's alleged that Morgan used the money to make short-term loans to his affiliate borrowers at rates high enough to cover the 11% interest owed to his investors. Much of the money raised was then diverted to pay other investors in a Ponzi-like scheme.

It was also alleged that Morgan kept two sets of books, one with an accurate accounting and another that was provided to lenders (required) for the servicing and refinancing of loans.

How These Ponzi-Schemes Were Being Perpetrated

Morgan and his associates had allegedly provided false information to those entities to obtain larger loans than they would have otherwise received on the multiple properties. The SEC believed Morgan had submitted fraudulent construction contracts and invoices that inflated payments to contractors. In addition, the misleading information included make-believe or fake contracts for property purchases that never occurred.

Chapter 5

Financial Ratios and Due Diligence

In this chapter, we will discuss financial ratios using an approach different from what has been taught in most college-level accounting courses. The goal is not to teach CPA coursework, but to equip the reader with the tools necessary to detect suspicious activity or even fraud in both a company's financial statements and transactions. Most accountants (CPA's) will audit for correctness. In contrast, Fraud Examiners look for irregularities to include abnormal reporting changes from one period to another.

While it's necessary to gather an understanding from both the borrower and seller's financial statements as to their respective company's operating performance; it's equally as important to know the makeup and meaning behind each ratio and that the numbers presented are true and accurate.

The goal of financial due diligence as it relates to commercial real estate is to ensure that all parties to include the lender, developer, buyer, and seller have received truthful and accurate information; and have not been misled by a misrepresentation of earnings, falsely reported expenses, inflated asset values and so forth.

Comparison

One of the best ways of performing financial analysis is to compare two (preferably three) years of financial statements. Take notice of any major swings or changes especially from totals of assets, liabilities or capital. Changes greater than 10% and $10,000 (a common rule of thumb used by accountants) require further investigation and inquiry as to why the changes may have occurred. In addition, changes that did not meet existing trends or in fact provided losses need to be investigated as well.

The job of the Accountant is to confirm the accuracy of reporting versus the Fraud Examiner whose job it is, to find out why.

Create a Checklist

At the beginning of the lender's risk assessment, financial ratios will need to be determined. The creation of a checklist at the outset can save analytical time if the borrower proves to not meet the organization's lending criteria.

It is strongly advised that the underwriter have a familiarity with the specific industry the borrower is engaged in, as each industry has its own peculiarities relating to accounting practices. Companies of one industry may be known to pay their bills every 30 days while others like those who manufacture items for the government find 90 days the norm. Acceptable business and accounting practices relating to custom window manufacturers (building on demand) will differ greatly from those industries involved in the consignment of inventory. Having this knowledge will lead to a better understanding of acceptable standards (ratios) and norms for that industry, resulting in time saved.

For example, each industry has its own characteristics. The average profit margins vary: While advertising has a net margin of 6.04%, the alcohol industry has a net margin of 19.13%. Similarly, computer services can expect to make 6.02% profit, while farming/agriculture hovers around 3.18%. Many key financial ratios can be found by visiting Dun & Bradstreet on the web or through various local sources.

While many financial ratios are provided in this text, every checklist should at a minimum consider the following four financial ratios:

Profit Margin (net income/sales). The first thing to ask, Is the borrower making money? Every lender wants to know whether borrowers are turning a profit or losing money. A serious profitability analysis includes a hard look at individual line items: such as returns, rent, payroll, owner compensation, travel and entertainment, depreciation and interest expense. This data when assembled provides important and relevant information regarding the borrower's financial health.

Why include depreciation in the formula? We do this because the larger the depreciation expense is in a year, the lower the company's reported net income—or its profit. However, because depreciation is a non-cash item, the expense doesn't change the company's cash flow.

Is the borrower's company making money or not?

Current Ratio (current assets/current liabilities). The current ratio measures the short-term (less than 1 year) liquidity or whether a company's current assets (including cash, receivables, and inventory) are ample to cover its current obligations (accrued expenses, payables, current debt maturities). In volatile markets, most lenders prefer a business with high liquidity, proving they have the wherewithal to sustain operations for an extended period.

Most lenders prefer a business with high liquidity.

Total Asset Turnover (total asset turnover (sales/total assets) is the barometer of the company's overall efficiency. The Total Asset Turnover measures the operation's efficiency by evaluating the sum or total dollar amount of sales generated from each dollar invested in assets. The posting of a low (TAT) may signal the business is incurring hardship in the collection of its receivables, while the (TAT) average across most industries is 4-6 turns. Besides, incurring possible hardship, a low (TAT) can signal an obsolete inventory.

A high TAT ratio suggests the company is performing well and is active in the collection of its receivables.

In cases where the valuation of inventory is important, it's imperative for the lender to request a copy from a recent audit of the borrower's inventory. Periodic inventory audits are conducted on a three to six-month basis. Important to know is whether the inventory audit was conducted in-house or by an outside (independent) firm as differences in opinion can exist. On a side-note, it would not be the first time that empty or near-empty boxes were found during an inventory audit.

What is the current status of the inventory? When was the last inventory audit conducted?

Interest Coverage Ratio (earnings before interest and taxes/interest expense) is a calculation that provides a "snapshot" of a company's current ability to pay interest charges. The higher the ratio, the better position the company is in to weather financial difficulties.

How is the company positioned to weather financial difficulties?

While the examination of financial statements is imperative in assessing a potential borrower, they alone are not a substitute for thorough due diligence. Proper due diligence means getting in and inspecting all aspects of the company's operations. Ask yourself: Is the company operating on par with current economic and industry conditions? Does management have sufficient experience? Is the company well organized? Do they have the collateral?

As a lender, one must be able within reason to accurately evaluate the borrower's financial status and minimize risks. By looking at many of the traditional financial ratios from a fraud examiner's point of view, the reader after some practice should develop a sense of where to look, what to look for and decide when further examination is warranted.

The goal of financial due diligence is to ensure all parties to include the lender, developer, buyer, and the seller have not been misled...

Financial Ratios Commonly used in Commercial Real Estate

In addition to financial ratios as they relate to accounting, it's important to review several of the ratios used by lenders in their preliminary analysis.

Capitalization Rate (Cap Rate)

The Capitalization Rate is the rate of return on a real estate investment (property) based on the income that the property is expected to generate. The capitalization rate or cap rate as it's called is used to estimate the investor's potential return on his or her investment.

Capitalization Rate = Net Operating Income / Current Market Value

Debt Coverage Ratio (DCR)

The Debt Service Coverage Ratio (DSCR) is defined as the net operating income divided by the total debt service. For example, the Net Operating Income (NOI) from the building is $185,000 per year and total amount needed to service the debt is $125,000 per year.

The DCR would then be: $185,000 / $125,000 or 1.48

Loan to Value (LTV)

The Loan-to-Value (LTV) is a term commonly used by lenders to express the ratio of the loan amount to the overall value of the building or property being purchased. The LTV represents the ratio of the mortgage as a percentage of the total appraised value of real property.

Mortgage Amount of $2,950,000 / Appraised Value of $4,500,000 = 65% LTV

Net Operating Income (NOI)

Net Operating Income (NOI) is the net amount of revenue or cash generated from the income property less the total amount of operating expenses. Remember, when calculating operating expenses, it is important to exclude the amounts called upon for debt service, leasing commissions, tenant improvements, repairs, taxes, depreciation and mortgage interest expense.

Total Gross Income – Total Expenses = Net Operating Income

When calculating the Net Operating Income (NOI), lenders will generally apply a percentage of income towards the "Vacancy and Credit Loss Allowance." This is common, even if the property is fully leased. Even though the borrower may manage the property themselves, the bank or lender in its calculations will almost always include a property management fee. The lender does this in order to cover the expenses involved should they need to regain control of the property. If having to do so, the lender will often hire a property management firm or use a member of its own staff to act as the property manager.

Financial statements rarely include a "Maintenance Reserve" but don't be surprised if the lender adds a maintenance reserve of 2% to 3% of Gross Income to the operating expenses.

Cash on Cash Return

The Cash-on-Cash Return is the ratio of annual cash-flow before taxes divided by the total amount of cash invested.

Annual $$ of Income or $800,000 / Total $$ Investment or $4,000,000 = 20%

Operating Expense Ratio

The Operating Expense ratio is a measure of what it costs to operate (total operating expenses) the income property compared to the total amount of income that the property generates. The operating expense ratio or (OER) is calculated by dividing the property's total operating costs by its gross operating income.

Operating costs of $250,000 / Gross Operating Income of $1,100,000 or 22%

The OER or Operating Expense Ratio should be compared against those of similar building types and size to decide if the reported operating costs are realistic or manipulated. Operating expenses usually range from 35% to 45% or more of the Potential Gross Income and is often dependent on the condition of the building. Other variables such as location and climate should be taken into account as well.

The "Big Two" are a Good Starting Point

Horizontal Analysis

Financial due diligence should always begin with a side by side comparison of balance sheets from previous periods. The horizontal analysis also known for its trend analysis capabilities is a great tool for comparing like account groupings such as assets and liability accounts in addition to revenue and expense accounts. While dollar amounts will most definitely be different, it's the percent change from one period to the next that is of interest.

Though the horizontal analysis is useful for identifying trends, the analysis can also lead to the discovery of fictitious revenues being reported. An indicator of such would be finding a significant increase in sales from previous periods along with matching increases in accounts receivable. The sudden increases may or may not be fraudulent in nature, but they are at a minimum worthy of further examination.

It's the percent changes from one period to the next that is of the most interest.

Vertical Analysis

Unlike the horizontal analysis which is primarily used to compare balance sheet items from previous periods, the vertical analysis investigates the relationships within the income statement and statement of cash flows.

The vertical analysis can be a great tool for exposing the operations of a company by assuming the % change from a group of transactions from one period to the next will have a similar effect on other items within the income statement. If not, find out why and in particular, what has led to the changes.

For instance, if x amount of sales generates y dollars in cost of Goods Sold or CoGS for one period, the percentage or result from the period examined should be similar for all periods. Though, not a hard and fast rule, but let's say, if $300,000 in sales generates a $75,000 in CoGS or 25% and the following period reports sales of $325,000, the CoGS should be in the neighborhood of $81,250 or 25%. If the reported CoGS is $95,000 or 29% we need to look for the reasons why. If anything, the CoGS should be less than 25%, not more due to the increased volume of sales. When differences occur like the one stated above, one should ask for an explanation.

Timing and both Horizontal & Vertical Analysis

There have been many a case where companies attempting to impress its base of investors were discovered to have committed a timing fraud. The fraud is most often accomplished by postponing or delaying shipments of product to a later period and knowingly recognizing the sale as income prior to receiving payment. Companies found participating in this activity have committed violations of improper revenue recognition and are usually required to restate their revenues.

During the examination, I would suggest reviewing the company's invoicing, shipping documents, revenues and accounts receivable. Do the accounts share similarities? If not, remember to record if not investigate the exact reasons for why they do not.

In short, horizontal analysis makes straight across comparisons of numbers or amounts of different periods, while vertical analysis involves using the numbers as percentages of a total and comparing them to previous periods looking for significant changes.

Cash Flow Margin Ratio and the Operating Cash Flow Ratio

Both the cash flow margin ratio and the operating cash flow ratio are excellent tools when examining the borrower's statement of cash flows. The purpose of calculating these ratios from our standpoint is threefold;

- The ratios should serve to measure the company's ability to repay its current debt;

- The ability of the company to turn its sales into cash, and

- The ratio is extremely useful when looking for "inconsistencies" from one period to the next. What's needed is the confidence the reported numbers are not fraudulent. As so, the numbers were not "invented" and used to find favor with the lender.

The ratios are as follows:

Operating Cash Flow Ratio

Cash Flow from Operations
    Current Liabilities

Measures a company's ability to pay current debt from the cash flow generated by operations.

Cash Flow Margin Ratio

Cash Flow from Operations
      Net Sales

The ability of a company to turn sales into cash.

	Year 1		Year 2	
Quick Ratio				
Cash + Securities + Receivables	195,000	2.05	215,000	1.00
Current Liabilities	95,000		215,000	

The Quick Ratio or as it's better known, the Acid Test Ratio is useful in determining if fictitious accounts receivables have been added to inflate sales. The ratio calculation will appear abnormally high and there will not be an offsetting of currently liability.

Activity Ratios

Activity ratios tell us how quickly the borrower's business converts its assets into cash or sales. Does the inventory sit on the shelves for months or is it being shipped to customers on a regular basis? The activity ratios help us to determine how effectively the borrower uses its assets. Meaning, is the borrower experiencing an increased level of sales or is the company in a slump?

Receivables Turnover

Net Sales on Account	250,000	1.61	450,000	2.14
Average Net Receivables	155,000		210,000	

If the fraud involves fictitious sales, the reported income is fake and will never be collected. As a result, the turnover of receivables will decrease.

Collection Ratio

365	365	226.30	365	170.33
Receivable Turnover	1.61		2.14	

The collection ratio is used to detect fictitious receivables stemming from larceny and skimming schemes.   Normally, this ratio will stay pretty consistent, but when it doesn't, it could be fraud or possibly a change in billing policies and collection efforts.

Inventory Turnover

Cost of Goods Sold	125,000	1.92	300,000	2.31
Average Inventory	65,000		130,000	

If the Cost of Goods Sold has increased due to theft of inventory, then this ratio will be abnormally high. It's also a possibility that an embezzlement is buried within the inventory account. Either way, a recommendation for a physical count of the inventory is encouraged.

Average Number of Days Inventory

$\dfrac{365}{\text{Inventory Turnover}}$	$\dfrac{365}{1.92}$	190.10	$\dfrac{365}{2.31}$	158.17

Purchasing and receiving inventory schemes can also affect the ratio. False increases (or debits) to Cost of Goods Sold (COGS) will result in an increase of the ratio. Significant changes from one period to the next is a good indicator of possible fraudulent activity.

Leverage Ratios

Leverage ratios are valuable when examining financial statements for fraudulent valuations of debt obligations. Quickly translated, this means that a poor performing company may be under significant pressure to show solid positive earnings. If so, they are more likely than a financially healthy company to succumb to fraudulent activity.

A poor performing company that is under significant pressure to show solid positive earnings is more likely than a financially healthy company to succumb to fraudulent activity.

Debt-to-Equity and Fraud

In 2007, Efstathios Kirkos, Charalambos Spathis and Yannis Manolopoulos in their study of thirty-eight Greek manufacturing companies compared to thirty-eight other companies not possessing the characteristics to commit fraud to detect financial statement fraud (later known as Kirkos et al) found the median "debt to equity" ratios of companies to possess these results:

Of the 76 companies examined:

Higher debt to total assets:

Companies that did commit financial statement fraud	2.706
Companies <u>not suspected of fraudulent activity</u>	1.075

Median debt to total assets:

Companies that did commit financial statement fraud	0.629
Companies <u>not suspected of fraudulent activity</u>	0.437

In summary, the findings concluded that companies with higher "debt to equity" ratios were more likely to commit financial statement fraud.

Debt to Equity

$\frac{\text{Total Liabilities}}{\text{Total Equity}}$	$\frac{139,750}{130,000}$	1.075	$\frac{351,780}{130,000}$	2.706

Debt to Total Assets Ratio

$\frac{\text{Total Debt}}{\text{Total Assets}}$	$\frac{78,600}{180,000}$	0.437	$\frac{113,220}{180,000}$	0.629

Other Leverage Ratios

The increase in these ratios corresponds with a rise in accounts payable, a liability account. Sudden changes in this ratio may prompt an examiner to look for fraud.

Profit Margin

Net Income	15,000	0.06	(25,000)	-0.06
Net Sales	250,000		450,000	

This profit margin ratio should remain fairly consistent. As the fraud is committed, artificially inflated sales will not have an accompanying increase in the Cost of Goods Sold. The net income will be overstated and the ratio will be abnormally high. False expenses and fraudulent disbursements will cause an increase in expenses and a decrease in the profit margin ratio.

- Artificially inflated sales **will not have an accompanying increase** in the CoGS.

- False expenses and fraudulent disbursements **will cause an increase in expenses** and a **decrease in the profit margin ratio**.

Asset Turnover

Net Sales	250,000	0.76	450,000	1.06
Average Assets	330,000		425,000	

The increased number is representative of a greater use of assets.

Cash Realization Ratio

Operating Cash Flow
   Net Income

Reductions in net income and increases in cash flows create inconsistencies in how a company operates and warrant further investigation. Do not rush to a conclusion based the results of a single ratio. While the inconsistency itself suggests further examination, be advised the results may or may not be attributed to fraudulent activity.

Profitability Ratios

Profitability ratios while extremely important to shareholders are widely used to assess a business's current reported earnings compared to the expenses incurred during the same period. In fact, these ratios may be the deciding factor for a company interested in selling off one or more of its assets.

As an example:

Alpha Company's revenue is derived from its two divisions. The Airbag Production Group (APG) located in Los Angeles which during its first quarter reported $10,000,000 in gross revenue and the Brake Lever Production Group (BLPG) of Atlanta which reported similar revenues for the same period.

In doing so, APG incurred $3,000,000 of expenses in its quest to earn $10,000,000 while BLPG earning the same amount of revenue incurred a total of $2,500,000 or $500,000 less in expenses than APG, demonstrating that brake lever production in Atlanta was in fact more profitable. Because of geographical differences, further examination may be required of labor costs and taxes before any decision to invest further or sell can be made.

Profitability ratios are indicators of a company's performance and are best used when comparing product lines, division against division or by region.

Gross Profit

Sales – Cost of Sales
   Current Liabilities

The Gross Profit measures how efficiently a company uses both labor and supplies in the production process.

Gross Profit Margin

$$\frac{\text{Net Sales} - \text{Cost of Sales}}{\text{Net Sales}}$$

Significant changes or variations in this ratio may indicate potential fraud or accounting irregularities.

Stock Sales

$$\frac{\text{Ending Inventory}}{\text{Net Sales}}$$

A decrease in this ratio indicates either that inventory is shrinking in relation to sales or that sales are increasing without a corresponding increase in inventory.

Return on Equity

$$\frac{\text{Net Income}}{\text{Shareholder Equity}}$$

Investors including shareholders frequently use this tool as a measure in judging the worthiness of their investments. It's in the best interest of the company to maintain a high return on equity.

Liquidity Ratios

Liquidity ratios are used to measure the borrower's (company) ability to meet its short-term debt obligations using its short-term assets. In effect, the company may have to sell or liquidate some of its assets in order to meet its debt obligations.

Remember, short-term as used in financial statements are assets that can be converted to cash in a period of one year or less. Examples of which include: Cash and cash equivalents, accounts receivable, inventory, marketable securities, prepaid expenses and other liquid assets that can be readily converted to cash.

Current Ratio

Current Assets	270,000	2.84	365,000	1.70
Current Liabilities	95,000		215,000	

Embezzlement will cause the ratio to decrease. Willful concealment of liabilities will cause the ratio to appear more favorable. A billing scheme will usually result in a decrease of current assets. As such, a decrease in cash will cause the ratio to decrease.

Working Capital

Current Assets – Current Liabilities

Working capital is a measure of both the company's efficiency and its short-term health. Decreases in working capital from one period to another may signal underlying problems in its operation.

Working Capital Turnover

$$\frac{\text{Net Sales}}{\text{Current Assets – Current Liabilities}}$$

The Working Capital Turnover (WCT) ratio shows exactly how well a company is using its working capital to fund operations compared to sales generated from these operations. Large increases could signify revenue related fraud.

Working Capital Index

Current Year WC – Previous Year's WC

The Working Capital Index is a means of comparing changes in working capital from one period to another. Decreases from one year to another may indicate an underlying problem in the company's operations.

Owner Prepared Statements

Oftentimes, the borrower does not have audited financials and submits to the lender what they have from their own accounting program. Chances are the financial statements received may've been created by someone without an accounting background.

Always ask about the origin of "Owner Prepared Statements."

Performing due diligence in these instances involves paying close attention to the Net Operating Income or NOI. It is a possibility the financial statements have been manipulated in order to show the borrower in the best light. Evidence of such can include findings that the borrower had been postponing the reporting of expenses to a later period or leaving out certain expenses altogether.

It is imperative to analyze the Income and Expense Statements for their reasonableness and make needed adjustments before:

- Estimating the likely sale price of the business, or
- Before presenting the financial information to others.

When dealing with owner prepared financial statements, be aware of the possibility that the statements may be manipulated and unreliable.

Make it a routine part of your due diligence process to compare the company's prepared documents against the IRS filings to

include the Schedule C for the Sole proprietor and Single member LLC, K-1's for multimember LLC's or the IRS form 1120 for both S and C Corporate filers.

Proforma Statements

Proforma Statements are often presented by owners as financial statements. They are not! These projections are usually a blend of actual reported income and expenses from the previous year and increased to what they believe future results could be. However, to increase the reliability of the projections, ask for the financial statements from at least the previous two years (preferably three) and prepare the projections of your own.

When dealing with owner prepared financial statements, be aware of the possibility that the statements provided may've been manipulated and are often viewed as unreliable and suspect.

Chapter 6

Mathematical Models Used for Detecting Financial Statement Fraud

Mathematical models are extremely useful when faced with large data sets and a limited amount of time. While many of us are very good at what we do, performing certain mathematical analysis can be a daunting task and is something most of us would prefer left to others. Luckily, software applications using MS Excel as a platform allows users to input the data leaving the computer to quickly perform the analysis.

The objective of this book is to help the reader identify questionable areas that are in need of further examination. My recommendation has been in difficult cases, is to seek assistance from individuals who are competent in both the areas of financial statement fraud examination and/or accounting.

Mathematical Models

The three most commonly used mathematical models are:

- Benford's Law
- The Altman's Z Score
- The Beneish Model

Benford's Law is useful where companies are experiencing financial difficulty. For decades, there have been schemes involving the posting of fraudulent (false) journal entries to report income that has not yet been earned and/or delaying the posting of (expenses) entries to the accounts payable to later periods. This is primarily done by unscrupulous members of management to boost balance sheet ratios, (e.g. more assets, less debt)!

94

The Altman's Z Score has been a staple of banks for years and is a fast and easy way to determine the financial health of a borrower and/or their company. The Altman's Z Score can be a predictor of those likely to obtain bankruptcy protection.

The Beneish model which requires a background in financial accounting, is a great tool when there is a questionable representation of earnings usually seen with the sale of income-producing properties, manufacturing businesses or large facilities where financial records are sketchy.

Benford's Law (Used to Detect Fraudulent Journal Entries)

Applying Benford's Law can be a great starting point as the test requires a download from the borrower's Quickbooks or other accounting program. Examining the "Paid Invoice" file will immediately reveal questions regarding vendors who may be real, fictitious, or possibly even a relative of an employee.

The questions raised here may cause one to take a deeper look at vendor files for:

- Completeness: (Remember, PO Box addresses are NOT enough)
- Addresses of vendors who share similar addresses with current or past employees.

There are plenty of examples of shill (non-existent) companies having been created with the sole purpose of invoicing the real business in hopes of receiving payment for services that were never provided. Unlike products that can be traced or accounted for, most acts of fraud appear to originate from the billing of services. Using the case involving the city of Pasadena California for example, a fraudulent billing scheme lasted nearly ten years and was perpetrated by a city employee along with two others.

My advice to those examining financial statements is to make sure bank and credit card accounts are being reconciled on a regular (monthly) basis. If not, expect fraud to have occurred or will occur.

Many shill (non-existent) companies have been created with the sole purpose of invoicing other businesses in order to receive payment for services that were never provided.

The beauty of Benford's Law is that when running a year's worth of "Paid Invoices" against the "Expected Proportion" or EP, the results of such "finds" can be determined and graphed in minutes. From the anomalies or spikes on the chart, one could possibly discover multiple payments, resubmitted invoices or fraudulent payments made to a vendor who's really an employee.

One could possibly discover multiple payments, resubmitted invoices or fraudulent payments made to a vendor...

The results are known as the "Actual Proportion" (AP) are the number of times (or frequency, thereof) the pre-specified digits appear above the expected proportion line. In simpler words, the anomalies that spike above the EP stand out like a "sore thumb" and require further examination.

Back in 1881, Simon Newcomb, a mathematician observed a multi-digit number like 3128 was more likely to begin with a 1,2, or 3. Moving forward to the late 1920's, Frank Benford then a Physicist for General Electric realized the first digits in naturally occurring numbers were also more likely to begin with the lower digits 1,2, or 3 as opposed to 7,8, and 9. Benford concluded that a four-digit number beginning with the number 1, occurred 30.1% of the time. Using a logarithm he developed, Benford was able to calculate the frequency of when the second digit of a multi-digit number would occur and so on for numbers 3 through 9.

The Law though very effective, cannot be used on a set of random numbers, such as lottery numbers nor non-natural numbers, such as telephone and Social Security numbers. Negative numbers are also excluded from the data set.

Benford's Law is best expressed using a line chart. The line chart shows the frequency or "Expected Proportion" according to Benford's Law in comparison with the second line representing the actual proportion (AP) from the data set. For example, "Paid Invoices" from a company's books is used to name the data set. The auditor or fraud examiner then looks for significant anomalies or spikes rising above the expected proportion line suggesting fraud may be present warranting further examination.

The Z-Statistic

When looking at results from Benford's law, the Z Statistic is used to establish both upper and lower boundaries along the EP line of (+- 5%) reducing the number of records that do not conform to Benford's Law. The Z-statistic is a value used to measure the significance of deviations between the real data set compared to Benford's expected frequency, leaving the spikes to be investigated.

Successful Applications of Benford's Law

In 1988, Charles Carslaw was the first to use Benford's Law in the field of accounting and applied it to the reported earnings from a number of New Zealand firms whose numbers were not meeting the expected distribution. In fact, the firms were alleged to have rounded up their numbers. Thomas, another statistician applied the same tests to US companies in 1989 and found a similar pattern.

Mark Nigrini, PhD an Associate Professor and Chartered Accountant came along in 1995 writing his dissertation on the use of Benford's Law and its application towards identifying tax evaders. His work included studies relating to sales figures, insurance claims and expenses, and believed the numbers followed Benford's Law. In his book, Benford's Law: Applications for Forensic Accounting, Auditing, and Fraud Detection, Nigrini felt it was difficult for people to act randomly...making it reasonable to assume that these habits flow through to a set of numbers that we (might) invent or fabricate. So based upon these digital patterns, Nigrini believed that an individual utilizing Benford's Law could detect the possible overstatement or understatement of financial figures.

Of the five-digit tests, (First Digit, Second Digit, First Two Digits, First Three Digits and Last Two Digits) Nigrini cites that the "first two and three digit" tests tend to identify overused digit patterns that could be:

- Indicative of fraud
- The possibility of erroneous inputs
- Duplicate processing of the same invoice.

At the same time, the last two digits test could be used to:

- Identify fabricated or rounded numbers.

Make sure bank and credit card accounts have been reconciled on a regular basis. If not, expect misuse or fraud to have occurred or will occur.

Overall, Nigrini noted that Benford's Law could be used to analyze the digital frequency within data sets to identify possible errors, fraudulent disbursements, and biases. Examples where examinations utilizing Benford's Law is the most useful are:

- Double billing or fraudulent billing by vendors
- Multiple payments to the same vendor
- And payments made above or slightly below established thresholds.

Altman Z Score Plus (Used to Detect Companies likely to Experience Bankruptcy)

The Altman Z Score (Plus) is a formula used by creditors to measure the financial health of a company and serves as an indicator of those who may possibly file for bankruptcy protection. The higher the Z score the stronger the financial health of the company. The lower the score the higher the risk of bankruptcy.

NYU Stern finance professor Edward Altman, developed the Altman Z-score formula in 1967, and was first published in 1968. In 2012, Altman released an updated version called the Altman Z-score Plus that can be used to evaluate:

- Both public and private companies,
- Manufacturing and nonmanufacturing companies,
- U.S. and non-U.S. companies.
- Corporate credit risk.

The lower the Altman Z Score the higher the risk of bankruptcy.

Altman Z-Scores and the Financial Crisis

In 2007, Professor Altman was of the belief credit ratings of specific asset-related securities had been rated higher than they should've been. Using the method, he designed, the Altman Z-score indicated with a high degree of probability that many companies were at significant risk and may be headed for bankruptcy.

Altman examined companies with a B credit rating and found many in the sample to have a median Z-score of 1.81. This indicated to Professor Altman that firms above the median were properly rated and those below should have actually been rated less than "B." Altman believed the companies that had received lower scores were overrated. He later felt these same companies were experiencing financial distress and had a high probability of becoming bankrupt. His calculations led him to believe that a crisis would soon occur leading to a meltdown in the credit market.

Altman further believed the crisis would stem from corporate defaults, such as the meltdown witnessed in 2009 with the crash of mortgage-backed securities (MBS). Hundreds of corporations soon defaulted at the second-highest rate in history.

The Altman Z Score using the formula is calculated as follows:

$$Z\text{-Score} = 1.2A + 1.4B + 3.3C + 0.6D + 1.0E$$

The Altman Z Model comprises the following ratios:

      A = Working Capital /Total Assets

      B = Retained Earnings / Total Assets

      C = Earnings Before Income & Tax / Total Assets

      D = Market Value of Equity / Total Liabilities

      E = Sales / Total Assets

Beneish M Score (Used to Detect a Manipulation in Earnings)

The Beneish model is a mathematical model that uses financial ratios and eight variables to identify whether a company has manipulated its earnings. The variables are constructed from the data in the company's financial statements and, once calculated, create an M-Score to describe the degree to which the earnings have been manipulated. A misrepresentation of earnings most often occurs when a company is pressured by upper management or by its shareholders to outperform the reported results from a previous period.

In the case of commercial real estate, a misrepresentation of earnings most often occurs when the borrower's goal is to either sell the business for more than its true value or lower its overall tax liability.

M-Scores of -2.22 and -1.78

An M-Score of less than -2.22 suggests the company is not a manipulator. However, an M-Score greater than -2.22 raises a red flag and that the company is possibly a manipulator of earnings. The Beneish M Model examines current year numbers and compares them to the prior year. Now, if the M-Score is above -2.22, this would be definitely a red flag or indicator that possible earnings manipulations exist.

According to Professor Massod Beneish, using a Compustat database of businesses from 1982 to 1992, he was able to determine that if the M score was greater than -1.78, the probability of manipulated earnings to exist was equal to or greater than 76%.

The Beneish model is comprised of the following eight variables:

The Beneish model calculation consists of eight variables which are added together to achieve an M-Score for the company.

M-score = $-4.84 + 0.920(DSR) + 0.528(GMI) + 0.404(AQI) + 0.892(SGI) + 0.115(DEPI) - 0.172(SGAI) + 4.679(Accruals) - 0.327(LEVI)$

Days' Sales in Receivables Index (DSRI) is the ratio of days' sales in receivables versus the same numbers from the prior year.

Gross Margin Index (GMI): Measured as the ratio of gross margin versus that of the prior year. A firm with poorer prospects is more likely to manipulate earnings.

Asset Quality Index (AQI) Measured as the ratio of non-current assets other than plant, property and equipment to total assets. AQI is the ratio of asset quality versus prior year.

Sales Growth Index (SGI): Measures the ratio of sales versus prior year's sales. While sales growth is not itself a measure of manipulation, struggling companies are likely to find themselves under pressure to manipulate sales in order to keep up appearances.

Depreciation Index (DEPI) Is measured as the ratio of the rate of depreciation versus prior year. The depreciation rate in a given year equals is equal to depreciation/(depreciation + net PPE) where PPE is Property, Plant and Equipment.

Sales, General and Administrative Expenses Index (SGAI): Measures the ratio of SGA expenses against those of the prior year. This is used on the assumption that analysts would interpret a disproportionate increase in sales ratio as a negative signal about firm's future prospects.

Total Accruals to Total Assets (TATA) Total accruals are calculated as the percentage change in working capital accounts other than cash less depreciation to total assets. Working capital accounts includes cash, inventory, accounts receivable, accounts payable, the portion of debt due within one year, and other short-term accounts. In this case, the total accrual involves removing the cash account and the amount of depreciation from the total.

Leverage Index (LVGI): Measures the ratio of total debt to total assets versus the prior year. The ratio is intended to capture debt covenants or borrowing limitations put in place by a creditor, which violations thereof, often leads to a fraudulent reporting of earnings.

Again, debt covenants are agreements between a company and a creditor stating limits or thresholds for certain financial ratios that the company may not breach.

The Variables (financial ratios) Used in the Model are as Follows:

- Days Sales in Receivables Index

(DSRI) $\text{DSRI} = (\text{Net Receivables}_t / \text{Sales}_t) / \text{Net Receivables}_{t-1} / \text{Sales}_{t-1})$

- Gross Margin Index (GMI)

$\text{GMI} = [(\text{Sales}_{t-1} - \text{COGS}_{t-1}) / \text{Sales}_{t-1}] / [(\text{Sales}_t - \text{COGS}_t) / \text{Sales}_t]$

- Asset Quality Index (AQI)

$$AQI = [1 - (Current\ Assets_t + PP\&E_t + Securities_t) / Total\ Assets_t] / [1 - ((Current\ Assets_{t-1} + PP\&E_{t-1} + Securities_{t-1}) / Total\ Assets_{t-1})]$$

- Sales Growth Index (SGI)

$$SGI = Sales_t / Sales_{t-1}$$

- Depreciation Index (DEPI)

$$DEPI = (Depreciation_{t-1} / (PP\&E_{t-1} + Depreciation_{t-1})) / (Depreciation_t / (PP\&E_t + Depreciation_t))$$

- Sales General and Administrative Expenses Index (SGAI)

$$SGAI = (SG\&A\ Expense_t / Sales_t) / (SG\&A\ Expense_{t-1} / Sales_{t-1})$$

- Leverage Index (LVGI)

$$LVGI = [(Current\ Liabilities_t + Total\ Long\ Term\ Debt_t) / Total\ Assets_t] / [(Current\ Liabilities_{t-1} + Total\ Long\ Term\ Debt_{t-1}) / Total\ Assets_{t-1}]$$

- Total Accruals to Total Assets (TATA)

$$TATA = (Income\ from\ Continuing\ Operations_t - Cash\ Flows\ from\ Operations_t) / Total\ Assets_t$$

Results of Those Likely to Commit Earning Manipulations

Data Analytics and Fraud Detection

Data analytic software can be useful when rooting out possible fraudulent transactions by searching for patterns, anomalies or trends. These can be duplicate entries of transactions, unusual ledger activity, asset misappropriation and above all, they could represent theft. Data analytics is essential when looking for dramatic changes when analyzing massive amounts of data from previous years.

Oftentimes, fraud examiners will use data analytics to respond early to "red flags" and can most often detect frauds before they're even noticed by others. Second, data analytics can be used to perform continuous monitoring to identify anomalies as they occur.

Below is a listing of areas where fraud has been encountered and is often detected using data analytics software:

Billing Schemes

- Unusual journal entries
- Duplicate payments
- Excessive purchases of items or an inordinate use of specific vendors

Check Tampering
- Out of range checks
- Questionable payee addresses
- Unusually high number of manual checks or checks made out to "Cash"
- Checks with no corresponding invoices

Payroll Schemes
- Multiple employees using the same SSN or bank account number for direct deposits.
- Manual payroll checks
- Employees with multiple pay increases
- Unsupported adjustments to gross or net pay
- Unusually high bonus payments
- Inappropriate wage levels given employees' "job classification"

Excessive Reimbursements
- Expenses submitted long after they were incurred
- Expenses that are consistently for the same amount
- Sequentially numbered receipts
- Cash payments for high dollar expenses

Cash Receipt Problems
- Unusually high number of voided transactions / refunds from retreats or gift shop sales.

- Invoices with partial payments when not the norm
- Unusual entries to cash accounts
- Debits or credits to unused accounts
- Users who access the accounting system at unusual times and dates (weekend).

One should never make a judgment or rely solely on the results of a single test.

Data Analytic software is not the "end all" in discovering fraud but definitely serves to narrow the search area providing a starting point of where to begin investigating. Please remember, the financial statement audit by itself "may guarantee" the accuracy of reporting but does little in the way of discovering fraud. In fact, the ACFE's 2014 "Report to the Nations" shows that less than 3% of fraud was uncovered by financial statement audits. Looking for fraud, think data analytics!

Conclusion

Financial due diligence plays an important role in the examination of commercial real estate transactions. It provides the investor with a "peace of mind" and knowledge that the information provided by others is solid (and in some cases not) regarding the income property's operational and financial performance.

Financial statements, in particular, convey the financial health of the subject property consistently. Material misstatements by management rarely occur. When they do, and rise to the level of fraud, it's usually because of a manipulation of accounting records and related supporting documents (evidence) which is often used to conceal the fraud.

Mark Nigrini, in the conclusion of his book Forensic Analytics; Methods and Techniques for Forensic Accounting Investigations writes "Fraud is here to stay. The only really surprising fact is that people are still surprised by the discovery of fraud."

Remember, no two properties are exactly alike. What appears at first glance to be suspicious may not be a fraud at all. However, any activity that is suspect should prompt further questioning to gain a clear understanding of the overall situation.

Information in this book as presented is valuable information derived from a variety of fraud-related resources. Again, the focus of this book is to bring awareness to the importance of fraud detection and the necessity for proper due diligence. It's a lot cheaper to ask for advice than to become a victim. When in doubt, seek the advice of a due diligence professional.

Financial Due Diligence for Commercial Real Estate provides many of the tools necessary to help you know where to look, what information is useful and the warning signs of fraud in determining if and where a problem may exist.

Appendix

Exhibit A

Signed Financial Statements from Borrowers and Guarantors to Include:

- ☐ Annual and quarterly financial information for the past three years
- ☐ Profit and Loss Statements
- ☐ Operating Statements
- ☐ Rent Rolls
- ☐ Audit results for the past five years
- ☐ Tax Returns for the past three years
- ☐ Balance Sheets
- ☐ Accounts Receivable
- ☐ Accounts Payable
- ☐ Asset Values
- ☐ Borrower's Income Projections
- ☐ Liabilities to include existing loans
- ☐ UCC Records
- ☐ Capital Structure
- ☐ Legal and related matters
- ☐ Project / Financial Projections
- ☐ Project / Market Analysis

Other Items that are Part of the Due Diligence Process Include:

- ☐ Evidence that property taxes are not in arrears
- ☐ Property pledged as collateral must have parcel identification numbers to Include:
- ☐ Legal description, and
- ☐ They are not subject to a parcel split.
- ☐ Phase I environmental report that is current and does not state that further action or review is warranted.

Red Flags to be on the Lookout for Include:

- ☐ Delinquent real estate taxes
- ☐ Declining sales prices or rental rates
- ☐ Cancellations in sales contracts or reservations
- ☐ Liberal concessions to include free rent, moving allowances, tenant improvement allowances, etc.
- ☐ Slow absorption or rent up of spaces in new projects
- ☐ Delinquent lease payments from major or anchor tenants
- ☐ Upward trending higher vacancy and turnover rates

Exhibit B

Red Flags (Warnings or dangers of a problem)

- ☐ Finding charges for non-allowable costs
- ☐ Failure to deliver contracted scope
- ☐ Lost Incentives and credits
- ☐ Overcharging for labor and materials
- ☐ Overpriced change orders

Risk Factors (Coming from sources both internal and external to the organization)

- ☐ Bonuses for estimators, project managers, purchasing agents and supervisors which is dependent on specific criteria.
- ☐ Tax-motivated income or loss goals
- ☐ Ownership dispute, potential sale, divorce
- ☐ Owner expectation and demand for income
- ☐ Manipulation of contract schedule
- ☐ Disregard for authority or regulations
- ☐ Continued employment of under-qualified accounting personnel
- ☐ Frequent change in external auditors
- ☐ Frequent or recent change in banking or bonding
- ☐ Inability of management to accurately project gross profit in the past
- ☐ Presence of OSHA fines and/or no safety program
- ☐ Pressure to meet loan covenants or bonding equity requirements
- ☐ Cash flow difficulties
- ☐ Interest rates on current debts higher than the industry average
- ☐ Significant claims or unapproved change orders
- ☐ Contractor that collects or uses significant amounts of cash
- ☐ Lack of owner or management oversight
- ☐ Inadequate recordkeeping over company procedures

- ☐ Lack of appropriate procedures for authorizing and approving transactions

Reducing these risks is Accomplished by:

- ☐ Conducting Weekly Budget Reviews
- ☐ Periodic Review by a Qualified Construction Auditor / Consultant

Exhibit C

Financial Ratios used in Commercial Real Estate

Capitalization Rate	$\dfrac{\text{Net Operating Income}}{\text{Current Market Value}}$
Debt Coverage Ratio (DCR)	$\dfrac{\text{Net Operating Income}}{\text{Total Debt Service}}$
Loan to Value (LTV)	$\dfrac{\text{Mortgage Amount}}{\text{Appraised Value}}$
Net Operating Income (NOI)	Total Gross Income − Total Expenses
Cash on Cash Return	$\dfrac{\text{Annual \$\$ of Income}}{\text{Total \$\$ Investment}}$
Operating Expense Ratio	$\dfrac{\text{Operating costs}}{\text{Gross Operating Income}}$

Vertical Analysis

Operating Cash Flow Ratio	$\dfrac{\text{Cash Flow from Operations}}{\text{Current Liabilities}}$
Cash Flow Margin Ratio	$\dfrac{\text{Cash Flow from Operations}}{\text{Net Sales}}$

Quick Ratio

$$\frac{\text{Cash + Securities + Receivables}}{\text{Current Liabilities}}$$

Activity Ratios

Receivables Turnover

$$\frac{\text{Net Sales on Account}}{\text{Average Net Receivables}}$$

Collection Ratio

$$\frac{365}{\text{Receivable Turnover}}$$

Inventory Turnover

$$\frac{\text{Cost of Goods Sold}}{\text{Average Inventory}}$$

Leverage Ratios

Average Number of Days Inventory

$$\frac{365}{\text{Inventory Turnover}}$$

Debt to Equity

$$\frac{\text{Total Liabilities}}{\text{Total Equity}}$$

Debt to Total Assets Ratio

$$\frac{\text{Total Debt}}{\text{Total Assets}}$$

Profit Margin

$$\frac{\text{Net Income}}{\text{Net Sales}}$$

Asset Turnover   Net Sales
                                                        Average Assets

Profitability Ratios

Cash Realization Ratio   Operating Cash Flow
                                                         Net Income

Gross Profit   Sales – Cost of Sales
                                                       Current Liabilities

Gross Profit Margin   Net Sales – Cost of Sales
                                                          Net Sales

Stock Sales   Ending Inventory
                                                          Net Sales

Liquidity Ratios

Return on Equity   Net Income
                                                      Shareholder Equity

Current Ratio   Current Assets
                                                      Current Liabilities

Working Capital   Current Assets – Current Liabilities

Working Capital Turnover $$\frac{\text{Net Sales}}{\text{Current Assets} - \text{Current Liabilities}}$$

Working Capital Index   Current Year WC − Previous Year's WC

About the Author

In 1984, Jerry Ipsen earned his B.S. in Business Administration from Oklahoma Wesleyan College (aka Bartlesville Wesleyan College) where he went on to serve as a Marine Corps Officer.

Following graduate school at Woodbury University and earning his MBA, Jerry began writing business plans and has done so for over $800 million in projects ranging from those as small as service stations to office buildings, residential complexes, hotels and even resorts. For the past 20 years, Jerry has been involved in commercial real estate.

Beside writing business plans, Jerry worked for Washington Mutual as a Senior Loan Consultant specializing in the loan origination of retail, office and industrial properties in Southern California. After that, he traveled out of the country conducting due diligence on several commercial projects.

In 2015, Jerry became a Certified Fraud Examiner specializing in financial due diligence as it relates to commercial real estate lending.

Jerry and his wife enjoy travelling and together they have five children and nine grandkids. He enjoys fishing and archery.

Bibliography

Abrams, Mark (2018) *Be Aware of These Real Estate Fraud Schemes*   Smith & Howard

ACFE *Report to the Nations*, 2014, 2016 and 2018

Andrews, Jeff (2018) Curbed.com; Real Estate News: *Why financial criminals use real estate to launder money*

Blackburne, George (2018) Info.c-loans.com: <u>*Commercial Loans and Rent Roll Fraud*</u>

Brown, Gregory (2017) *Can you Sue a Contractor for Using Substandard Materials?*

Cho, Gustan (2019) Gustancho.com: *How to Avoid Mortgage Fraud During Mortgage Process*

Commercial Real Estate Lending*: Comptrollers Handbook Safety and Soundness* (2013) Office of the Comptroller of the Currency

Delston, Ross, Legal Executive Institute (2018) *Real Estate Fraud: A Money Laundering Challenge for Financial Institutions*

Grassano, Bill (2011) *Commercial Real Estate Financing Fraud:* Financial Crimes Enforcement Network

Guerin, Jessica (2019) Housingwire.com: *Top U.S. landlord charged with running Ponzi scheme in massive multifamily mortgage fraud probe*

Harzler, Lisa Harms (2018) *Seller's representative and agency liable for fake wire transfer instructions*   Sorling Northrup Attorneys

What is commercial Real estate fraud? Jackson Law Firm (2015)

Johnson, Paul J. (2010) *Real Estate Legal Due Diligence: Look Before You Leap* Shannon, Gracey, Ratliffe & Miller, LLP

Kranacher, Mary-Jo, Riley, Richard A. Jr, Joseph T. Wells (2011) *Forensic Accounting and Fraud Examination* John Wiley & Sons

Lane, Ben for the Wall Street Journal (2018) *Inside the scandal that could explode multifamily real estate; WSJ reports on massive multifamily mortgage fraud investigation*

Mantone, Pamela S. (2013) *Using Analytics to Detect Possible Fraud: Tools and Techniques* John Wiley & Sons

Martin, Vernon (2011) *Real Estate Transaction Fraud Prevention Checklist: Fraud Prevention for Commercial Real Estate Valuation*

Mortgagefraudblog.com (2015) *New York Businessman Pleads Guilty in Multi-Family Fraud*

Mroski, Bob (2011) *Financial Statement Fraud Casebook: Baking the Ledgers and Cooking the Books*

Myhre, Dennis (2106) *Money Laundering in Commercial Real Estate* Fiduciaryfactor.com

Nigrini, Mark J. PhD (2011) Forensic Analytics*: Methods and Techniques for Forensic Accounting Investigations* John Wiley & Sons

Nigrini, Mark J. PhD (2012) Benford's Law*: Applications for Forensic Accounting, Auditing and Fraud Detection* John Wiley & Sons

Plate Ltd (2017) Project Funding/Due Diligence

Podkul, Cezary for the Wall Street Journal (2018) *U.S. Pursues One of the Biggest Mortgage-Fraud Probes Since the Financial Crisis*

Podkul, Cezary for the Wall Street Journal (2019) *SEC Accuses Major U.S. Landlord of Running 'Ponzi Scheme-Like' Scam*

Realtor Magazine (2019) *Worldwide Crackdown on Money Laundering in Real Estate*

Ryan, Terry of Proofpoint for Bisnow (2018) *Real Estate Companies A Top Target for Email Fraud*

Smith, Russell *Real Estate Wire Fraud Is Rampant. Realtors, Buyers, Sellers, Lenders, and Attorneys Beware!*   OVM Financial

Stribling, Dees (2018) Bisnow National "Real Estate Companies A Top Target For Email Fraud"

Texas National Title (2018) *Real Estate Agent and Broker are Found Liable for Wire Fraud Loss*

Willis, Marvin (2018) Smith & Howard: *Due Diligence Matters*

Wood, Meredith (2019) for Fundera, Inc. *Profit Margin: Formula and What Makes a Good Profit Margin*

Wright, James (2018) Consultant, US Army War College. *Dirty Money: Development, Money Laundering, & Real Estate*

Yale, Aly J. (2019) Forbes Magazine *Real Estate Wire Fraud Is Real -- And It Almost Happened to Me.*

Zack, Gerard M. (2013) *Financial Statement Fraud: Strategies for Detection and Investigation*   John Wiley & Sons

Zimmer, Joanie L. (2019) Amrock.com *10 Tips for Countering Wire Fraud in Commercial Real Estate*

CPSIA information can be obtained
at www.ICGtesting.com
Printed in the USA
LVHW040908111119
636959LV00003B/964